JOHN RAREY
HORSE TAMER

JOHN RAREY HORSE TAMER

HORSE TAMER

Nancy Bowker

J. A. ALLEN: LONDON

British Library cataloguing-in-publication data
A catalogue record for this book is available from
the British Library

ISBN 0.85131.663.8

Published in Great Britain in 1996 by
J. A. Allen & Company Limited
1, Lower Grosvenor Place
London, SWIW OEL

Typeset in Hong Kong by Setrite Typesetters Ltd
Printed in Hong Kong by Dah Hua Printing Press Co. Ltd

Edited by Susan Beer
Designed by Nancy Lawrence

To my daughter Jessica, that she may light the candle of kindness to animals in the next generation.

To my father Jim Souder, for awakening the love of art, of life, in so many.

To my husband Russ, for his steady support and assistance; and to the memory of his wonderful mother, Dorothy Bowker.

CONTENTS

$\mathscr{A}$CKNOWLEDGMENTS

The author wishes to acknowledge the generous help of the following:

In America:

Madelyn Larsen, Senior Editor, Howell Book House, New York; Elsie and William H. Rarey; Richard and Mary Lee Lowe; The Ohio Historical Society: Gary Arnold, Alfred Howard, Kim Feinknopf, Melinda Knapp, Alice Raunchon, the staff of the Archives/Library; and John Barsotti, Historian; The Racquet and Tennis Club Library, New York: Gerard J. Belliveau, Jr, Librarian, and Todd Thompson, Assistant Librarian; Anne and Ed Rarey; Robin Rivello; Pat Roberts; Laura Rose, Librarian, National Sporting Library; Marianne Souder: my mother, whose example of perseverance has always been an inspiration; Timothy Souder: for lending his computer genius beyond the call of brotherhood; Stuart Thayer, past president, The Circus Historical Society; Carol Schultz Vento: for her wonderful friendship; Melinda Wardwell: for help along the way

In England:

J. A. Allen & Co., London: Editors Caroline Burt, Elizabeth O'Beirne-Ranelagh, and Susan Beer; British Library, London: G. Ridgley, Librarian; Epsom Grand Stand Assoc., Surrey; T. P. Neligan; Guildhall Library, London: R. M. Harvey, Research Librarian; Household Cavalry, Chelsea Barracks, London: David Smith; Royal Archives, Windsor Castle: Pamela Clark, Deputy Registrar; The Royal Commission on Historical Manuscripts, London: G. H. Mandelbrote, Curatorial Officer, Westminster City Archives; Victoria Library, London: M. J. Swarbrick, Archivist

And gratefully to acknowledge the invaluable assistance of the following Libraries, Historical Societies, Institutions and Museums:

Academy of Music, Philadelphia, Pennsylvania: Jo Anne E. Barry, Archivist; Boston Public Library, Boston, Massachusetts: Charles S. Longley, Curator of Microtexts and Newspapers; Bridgeport Public Library, Bridgeport, Connecticut: Diane Kurtz, Historical Collections; Burlington County Library, Westampton, New Jersey; The Chicago Public Library, Chicago, Illinois: Kristin Lipkowski, Ref. Librarian; Cinnaminson Branch Library, Cinnaminson, New Jersey; Circus World Museum, Baraboo, Wisconsin: Fred Dahlinger, Jr, Director, Parkinson Library and Research Center; Cleveland Public Library, Cleveland, Ohio: Joan Clark, Head of Main Library; Columbus Metropolitan Library, Columbus, Ohio: Olivia P. Riley, Librarian; Daily Racing Form, Hightstown, New Jersey: George Bernet, Editor; Dallas Public Library, Dallas, Texas: Gerald Schroeder, Texas History; Danbury Public Library, Danbury, Connecticut: Diana Nolan, Ref. Librarian; Dittrick Museum of Medical History, The Cleveland Medical Library Assoc., Cleveland, Ohio: Jennifer K. Simmons, Collections Manager; Enoch Pratt Free Library, Baltimore, Maryland; Franklin County Genealogical Society, Columbus, Ohio; Franklin County Historical Society, Columbus, Ohio: Denny Jay, Office Manager, Ted Kessel, History Supervisor; Fredericksburg and Spotsylvania National Military Park, Fredericksburg, Virginia: Donald Pfanz, Staff Historian; Free Library of Philadelphia, Philadelphia, Pennsylvania; Groveport Township Office, Groveport, Ohio: Julie Fisher; Hussian School of Art, Philadelphia, Pennsylvania: Ronald Dove, Ms Adams; Illinois State University, Milner Library, Normal, Illinois: Bret A. Heim, Ref. Librarian; Library of Congress, Washington, DC; Maryland Historical Society, Baltimore, Maryland: Helen Burns, Library Assistant; Metropolitan Toronto Reference Library, Toronto, Ontario: Gwen Ing, Librarian; National Air and Space Museum, Smithsonian Institute, Washington, DC: Tom D. Crouch, Chairman, Aeronautics Dept.; National Archives, Washington, DC: Michael T. Meirer, Military Ref. Branch; New Haven Colony Historical Society, The Whitney Library, New Haven, Connecticut; James W. Campbell, Librarian; Norwalk Museum, Historical Research Library, Norwalk, Connecticut: Joan Robidoux, historian; The Ohioana Library, Columbus, Ohio: Barbara Maslekoff, Librarian; Ohio Wesleyan University, Beeghly Library, Delaware, Ohio: Catherine N. Schlichting, Curator, OWU Collection; Public Library of Cincinnati and Hamilton County, Cincinnati, Ohio: Patricia M. Van Skaik, Head of the History Dept.; Russell Library, Middletown, Connecticut: Denise Mackey-Russo, Ref. Librarian; Texas State Library,

Austin, Texas: Laura K. Saegert, Archivist; University of Illinois at Urbana-Champaign, Urbana, Illinois: William McClellan, Head of the Music Library; The Western Reserve Historical Society, Cleveland, Ohio: Ann K. Sindelar, Ref. Supervisor; White Sulphur Springs, West Virginia: Chamber of Commerce; The Greenbrier, White Sulphur Springs, West Virginia: Robert Conte, Historian; Willard Hotel, Washington, DC: Ann McCracken, Public Relations; The Woodman Institute, Dover, New Hampshire: R. A. Whitehouse

And a sincere Thank You to:

Madeline and Lee Bondy, Russell Bowker Sr, Brenda, Joseph & Heather Ciribassi, Dr Sharon Cregier, Alice Dunn, James Dunn and Family, Susan Dunn and Family, Barbara Eustis-Cross, Anna Guitton DVM, Beverly Haaf, Anna Hageman, Josephine Haworth, Judy Hyslop, Susan Smith James, Lyn Kamer, Carol Lang, Judy Lewis, Dina Leacock, Phyllis Misko, Laurie, Karl, Molly and Charlotte Pfeifer, Mary Regler and the Double R Special Riders, Michael & Treenie Roads, Caroline Robbins, Marlene Sanderson, Margaret Seaman, Alice Sidener, Penelope Smith, Linda Tellington-Jones, Betty and Kevin Thornell, Matthew Valosen, Rosemary and Frank Vento, Marie and Doug Wardwell, Tom, Pat, Kelly and Tommy Whalen, Pat Williams, Sylvia Williams

$\mathcal{I}$NTRODUCTION

$\mathcal{J}$OHN Rarey came out of the pages of history and into my mind with the urgency of his message. At the time, I was writing a book about wild horses with Barbara Eustis-Cross, and researching the different methods used to handle them.

While reading *The Horsemasters* by Josephine Haworth, I was fascinated by the account of a young quiet horseman in a top hat, John Rarey, who trained extremely dangerous horses in front of vast audiences. He travelled all over the world, handling the most aggressive horses that could be found. And his gift for understanding horses brought him the honour of appearing before some of the greatest women and men of the nineteenth century: Queen Victoria and Prince Albert; the Emperor Napoleon III in Paris; Czar Alexander II in St Petersburg, Russia; Charles Dickens; Alexander Von Humboldt; Ralph Waldo Emerson; and quite possibly Abraham Lincoln.

Rarey toured the major cities of Europe and America, travelling with his fiery dark stallion – who became as celebrated as he for his spirited performances. Rarey was acknowledged by many who saw him as the finest horseman of his age, and indeed he had unequalled courage and skill in handling vicious horses; yet the point which impressed me the most was his unflagging devotion to a cause.

This was his self-appointed quest, and of it he said:

My constant endeavor has been and will be in every exhibition I may conduct, to show to the world, and convince them by demonstrations,

1

that kindness, of all other means, is the best mode of training the horse.

For he believed, as he stated at a lecture in Baltimore, Maryland in 1861:

> There was no more reason for the violent breaking of a horse than for the violent breaking of a child. In either case, more was to be accomplished by the hand of gentleness than by any method of force human ingenuity had yet devised.

In Rarey's lifetime, spanning the middle of the 1800s, children were physically punished at home, in schools, and at factories; and for horses, many training methods were rough and unmerciful.

Horseman Dennis Magner, in his book *The New System of Educating Horses*, published in 1881, remarked: 'Boys and colts, so much alike in friskiness and stubbornness, both are misunderstood and abused in equal ratio. The boys are shaken and whipped, and colts are yanked, kicked, and pounded.'

This was the era portrayed by Charles Dickens in his classic novels, and also by Anna Sewell in *Black Beauty*. The Victorian age was described by those living then as nothing less than a 'hell for horses'.

In the book *Coaching Days of England*, Anthony Burgess wrote:

> The term 'to die in harness' comes from these times: in the summer of 1821 about 20 horses dropped dead on one mail route alone...A coachman had one concern only – to reach his destination on time – and he used the whip as the modern driver uses the accelerator...It was not the speed that killed them so much as weight – excess loads of merchandise which paid better than passengers.

Besides the dangers of dying from exhaustion, diseases also killed or disabled a lot of horses. Sickness ran like wildfire through livery stables, resulting in a constant turnover of new horses. There were epidemics of strangles, glanders, bronchitis, and influenza. Adding to the misery was a host of leg, skin, digestive, and eye problems: colic, laminitis, and ringworm; bowed tendons, bog spavin, capped hocks and cataracts, plus many others.

Captain M. Horace Hayes, author of veterinary and general books on horses, stated in *Among Men and Horses*, published in 1894, that he believed many horses became moon-blind from the ammonia in the stables. Hayes wrote of once examining four horses that were pulling a mail coach in Ireland. Out of all of them, there was only one eye capable of seeing – and that belonged to the one-eyed coachman.

Horses of all shapes and sizes literally turned the wheels of daily life: from tiny pit ponies in coal mines, to omni-bus and stagecoach horses, to the mighty Shires hauling tremendous burdens. Horse power was essential for business, transport, farm work, and pleasure, and it is difficult to understand the cruelty with which the animals were often treated. A shocking amount of outright abuse was even tolerated in public.

A reporter for the *Columbus [Ohio] Gazette* recorded on 15 December 1865 that 'Ponderous dray loads enough to kill the horse can be seen at any hour coming up heavy grades. Wagons loaded with stone, wood, lumber taxing the animal's strength to the utmost tension, some more like skeletons than live beasts, are urged and goaded onwards.'

In 1824, the Society for the Prevention of Cruelty to Animals was founded in London. It was given royal patronage (extending its initials to RSPCA) in 1840 by Queen Victoria, who had an encompassing tenderness for horses and all animals. While travelling up a steep hill in her carriage, the Queen would often request that the passengers get out and walk, to lessen the strain on the horses.

By the middle decades of the 1800s, the RSPCA's aims were gaining acceptance, but progress was slow. As the *Illustrated London News* commented on 24 April 1858, horses were starved, beaten, and overworked:

> – good simple man! – has contended himself with now and then venturing a word of mild remonstrance against 'cruelty to animals,' 'unnecessary violence', and 'eagerness of temper'. He has done no more, for he has known nothing more, except that the prevalent system was barbarous…the method has been simply this: thrash or curb them into obedience.

This statement was illustrated by J. B. Booth in his book, *Bits of Characters: A Life of Henry Hall Dixon,* regarding a mail coach horse called the 'Waterloo Mare'. This mare had formed the wearisome habit of always stopping and refusing to budge at the end of several miles. Booth writes:

> She accordingly left Penrith, and got a few miles in the Glasgow mail, when, according to her wont, she suddenly sulked, and sat down on

her haunches like a dog, with her forelegs straight out before her. The coachman got down, took a rail out of the hedge, and struck her nine times below the knee with the flat side of it. Such energetic treatment brought her to...

Many horses were ruined by such brutality, becoming crippled or vicious, or both. There were serious consequences too, for the people handling these traumatized horses. When the horse became aggressive or resistant, the only remedy many people knew was to threaten and then attack, hitting the horse or striking him with a whip to 'show him who's boss'. This never cured the problem, for many resistances were rooted in fear or pain, rather than stubbornness. And sometimes, using these warfare tactics turned into a fatal mistake.

There is a grim story in J. B. Booth's aforementioned book, taken from a column Henry Hall Dixon wrote, about a racehorse named Merlin.

> Tyler, the groom at Riddlesworth, was the only man who dare go up to him [Merlin], armed with an immense stick; and one unhappy day when another of the grooms, whom the horse especially hated, was called for, all that was known about him was that he had been seen going into the box.
>
> 'Mercy on us!' said Tyler, 'he's a dead man; that's the moan I heard as I passed there, ten minutes since!'
>
> And sure enough, the horse was kneeling on him, and fairly wallowing in his blood...He only lived two hours after he was got away, and Mr Thornhill settled a handsome pension on his widow.

Whether the account was exaggerated or not we can't say for sure, but it was a fact that grooms were on occasion killed by horses that had turned violent. A number of reasons drove horses into this sad state. There were acts of brutality done to them – such as those by one man who boasted he beat horses 'until they moaned', chronic pain; inherited irritability; impatient handling of those with a highly strung temperament; or the effects of constant confinement, such as many stallions had to undergo on racecourses and breeding farms.

What was the answer to this dangerous dilemma; how were such horses to be handled without risking life and limb? In the 1850s, 'after spending the labor of his life upon it', John Rarey believed he had found the answer: a system 'mild yet firm, which entirely does away with the system of rough breaking hitherto in vogue'.

Rarey's system involved a series of steps which did not harm the horse if done correctly, but expert skill, patience, and respect for the horse were required. The common practices of dealing with vicious horses were much more severe. The novelist Theophile Gautier, after seeing Rarey perform in Paris, wrote in the newspaper *Le Moniteur Universal*, 21 January 1860: 'What pleases me in the method of this American is that it is humane – no nose torture, no whip with cutting thongs, no spurs with sharp points, no posts of suffering, nothing but kindness – the moral victory.'

Another point Rarey emphasized in his lectures, other than the reclamation of angry horses, was the need for gentleness in the training of young horses. Many colts and fillies were started too early due to the cost of raising them, and their education rushed along, so they could be sold or used as soon as possible. Problems arose due to misunderstandings of the horse's inborn reactions, sensitivities, and fears.

A lot of young horses were not given the chance to get used to saddles, bridles, and harness gradually – to overcome their natural caution of anything new. Instead, some trainers put new equipment on and tightened it up right away. The frightened horses would explode into bucking, or panic and run. The shock and fears these situations caused, sometimes ruined the horse, or set up life-long resistances to working with people.

This was what happened particularly with wild horses, who were broken soon after capture. These methods were described by author and journalist Samuel Sidney, in an 1858 edition of Rarey's book, *The Art of Taming Horses*, which Sidney edited for him in London.

The Gauchos on the South American Pampas, lasso a wild horse, throw him down, cover his head with one of their ponchos, or cloaks, and, having girthed on him one of their heavy demi-piqued saddles, from which it's almost impossible to be dislodged, thrust a curb bit, capable of breaking the jaw with one tug, into the poor wretch's mouth, mount him with a pair of spurs with rowels six inches long, and ride him over the treeless plains until he sinks exhausted in a fainting state…

There is another milder method sometimes adopted by these Pampas horsemen…after lassoing a horse, they blind his eyes with a poncho, tie him fast to a post, and girth a heavy saddle on him. The animal sometimes dies at once of fright and anger: if not, he trembles, sweats, and would, after a time, fall down from terror and weakness.

Rarey spoke in his lectures about the futility of forcing something on a horse that it is afraid of. He told his audiences about a horse he knew when he was young, who always shied at the sight and smell of buffalo robes. The owner decided to get the horse over the fear by tying him up, and laying a buffalo robe over the horse. Unfortunately, when he threw the robe on, the horse was so overwhelmed with fear that it died instantly on the spot.

Rarey thought that this type of tragic error could be avoided, if people became aware of how horses think, and why they act the way they do. His belief in working with a horse's natural pattern of reactions, instead of against them, runs throughout his original book, published in Ohio in 1856, *The Modern Art of Taming Wild Horses*. In his advice for bringing an untrained horse from a field into a stable, Rarey writes:

> This should be done as quietly as possible so as not to excite any suspicion in the horse of any danger befalling him. The best way to do this is to lead a broken horse into the stable first and hitch him, then quietly walk around the colt, and let him go in of his own accord.
>
> It is almost impossible to get men who have never practised on this principle to go slowly and considerately enough about it. They do not know that in handling a wild horse, above all other things, is that good old adage true, that 'haste makes waste', that is, waste of time – for the gain of trouble and perplexity.
>
> One wrong move may frighten your horse, and make him think it necessary to escape at all hazards for the safety of his life – and thus make two hours work of a ten-minute job; and this would be all your fault, and entirely unnecessary – for he will not run unless you run after him, and that would not be good policy unless you knew that you could outrun him, for you will have to let him stop of his own accord after all. But he will not try to break away unless you attempt to force him into measures.

How these words rang true as I observed how, when people tried to force them into chutes, wild horses reacted by rearing and struggling to get out. And again, when my daughter Jessica and I spent an hour trying to catch our mustang Sierra in an open field when we first got her. Luring her with her friend – a well-trained mare – and standing very quietly with a handful of carrots, was the only way we were able to catch her.

While reading Rarey's book and the reports in newspapers about his lectures, the compassion and wisdom of his words really touched me. They echoed my beliefs about the aggressive training practices I've seen used against horses: rough sawing hands with severe bits, tight tie-downs, electric shocks, insurance killings, and administering drugs. I remember one racehorse who was given drugs to mask the pain of an injured leg. He was started in a race anyway, and apparently put all his weight on his bad leg and it gave way. His leg was shattered and he had to be put down.

I believe that Rarey may have felt this same anguish while witnessing the daily abuse carried on against horses in his day. He understood though, that the key to any type of reform was education, and this he sought to do with his performances.

He knew however that people would not sit still very long to be dryly lectured on being kind to horses. People were willing to learn, but they wanted it presented in an exciting package. Rarey solved this with a dramatic flare, by giving vivid proof of his message that 'kindness is power', by transforming 'equine savages' into calm cooperative horses before the eyes of the audience.

The session was no doubt frightening for the horse, being on stage in front of thousands of people. The changes in the horse's behaviour though, may have saved the lives of many aggressive horses, whose next step would have been the killer's yard.

Rarey had such skill and empathy for them while he was working, that eye witnesses noted how afterwards the horses would act as if they had affection for him. Samuel Sidney mentioned in his editor's remarks for Rarey's book, that Rarey's handling would:

> …render docile the most violent horses, but, most strange of all, inspire them with a positive confidence and affection after two or three lessons… 'How this is or why this is', Mr Langworthy, the veterinary surgeon to Her Majesty's stables, observed, 'I cannot say or explain, but I am convinced, by repeated observation on many horses, that it is a fact.'

The method Rarey used was very successful, and an improvement over the contemporary practices of training vicious horses, but it cannot be stressed strongly enough that it must not be used today; the risk of harm to the handler and the horse are too great. Safer methods are available now to achieve the same results of calm obedience and the development of trust. My goal therefore in the writing of this book was not to advocate Rarey's system of training for today, but rather to share his exciting adventures and his philosophy of using gentleness in working with all horses.

How can the life of a horseman who lived almost a century and a half ago, give us clues to the questions we struggle with today? Because, despite all the technological marvels that have come forth in the last 150 years, horses and humans have not changed very much. We are all born with the experience of millions of years of evolutionary responses programmed in our brains; so we think and react very closely to those of yesterday.

Therefore, we can learn a great deal by studying the mistakes, discoveries, and wisdom of the ages past. In the arts the foundation is laid by studying the masters – whether a musician studying Mozart, Beethoven, or Bach; or an artist seeking out the work of Rembrandt, Leonardo da Vinci, or Michelangelo.

Likewise, in the art of horsemanship, serious students study the thoughts and techniques of the master riders and trainers. As Samuel Sidney wrote in his book, *The Illustrated Book of the Horse,* published in 1875, that the 'man who learns nothing from the collected experience of the finest horsemen of the present and past generations must be a very poor or very conceited creature'.

And as Rarey reasoned in his book, 'What would be the condition of the world if all our minds lay dormant?' In action and in words, Rarey challenged his generation to use the higher qualities of their minds and hearts in training horses, rather than their anger, fists, and whips. In getting to know the ideas and life work of John Rarey, a question that has long disturbed me was answered. It is: do we have to accept the violence and abuse done to horses in the name of training, economics, or sport as just the way it is – or can we do something about it ? The answer I received was: we all have within us the power to speak up for what is right.

This is a message we need to hear again today, at a time when the violence of our age so often spills over to our horses, our children, and among ourselves.

1

EARLY DAYS IN OHIO

*T*HE arrival of a stage coach brought a wave of excitement to the Rarey's roadside inn. The rumble of hooves and the sound of the coachman's horn heralded new people, horses, and stories from afar. There were tales of hardship, danger, and humour, from the pioneer families moving west in Conestoga wagons; teamsters hauling loads to the markets; livestock drovers with cattle, pigs and sheep; and best of all, the colourful circus troupes with their wirewalkers, tumblers, bareback riders, and trick horses. While the horses were being unhitched and cared for, the stories would be told, or later on when the passengers and drivers were thawing out or cooling off in the tavern.

Adam and Mary Catherine (Pontius) Rarey had opened the inn around 1815. The road past their log home in Ohio was then only a dirt path through the woods to the city of Columbus, about ten miles away. Traffic increased as the road was improved, and the flow of settlers coming over the Allegheny Mountains grew year by year.

The Rarey's family grew steadily as well. When their son John Solomon Rarey was born on Thursday 6 December 1827, he became the caboose of the family – the eleventh child.

Another baby, a daughter, was born in 1830, but tragically she only lived a year. Epidemics of diseases carried many young ones away in these times. The Rareys mourned five children who did not live past early childhood. Their surviving children were: Margaret, William H., Elizabeth, Frederick, Charles, and John.

9

As the youngest, John must have been considered fondly, yet he endured a lot of loneliness. His parents, besides running the inn, were farming a large tract of land, and raising horses. There were no other young children around, for his brothers and sisters were much older, and all the neighbours lived at a distance.

Rarey turned for company to the work horses, and the colts and fillies growing up in their pastures. Spending so much time with them, he grew to appreciate their sense of fun and friendship. He was given his own pony at the age of four. Soon, he was carrying messages to the neighbours, and running errands for his mother on horseback. As he grew, he weathered the usual falls, bites and kicks that come with being around horses.

When he was nine years old, during a visit to town he had a harrowing adventure. His pony shied and took off, running pell mell through the village in a blind panic. Rarey clung to the saddle through the moments of mad galloping and the pony scrambling up and down deep ditches and through water. He made it back home still astride, gaining the respect of those who saw them dashing by, for his ability to stay calm in a dangerous situation. He put this quality to use when he began to try training the young horses on their farm. He first used the common method of saddle breaking, of climbing aboard and hanging on through the rodeo ride. The resulting bruises and broken bones inspired him to search for a more sensible way.

He watched how the horses acted in the pasture with other horses, and with cows and sheep; and realized they were friendly with those who offered no harm. He became certain that the key to training lay in first convincing the horses that they wouldn't be hurt. In the field, he tried a quietly patient, non-threatening approach, and found he could catch and halter horses that no one else could get near.

He also listened to the advice, horse sense and nonsense of other horsemen, farmers, and circus trainers, learning a little more from each one. The most crucial lesson though, came from his own sense of right and wrong. In the course of daily life, he often witnessed the brutal treatment many horses received: the beatings, the cruel use of bits and spurs, lame horses being worked, harness rubbing on raw sores, old sick horses abandoned in the woods, and stage horses dying from exhaustion.

The conviction grew steadily in him, that it was absolutely wrong to treat horses so unmercifully. And it became clear to him that using force was a backward approach to working with a sensitive, intelligent animal like the horse; for most horses would willingly cooperate if given half a chance. Many times too, when horses were punished for disobedience, it was the person at fault.

When bad tempered people tried to bully horses into doing things with shouts and the whip, the fear and excitement it caused immediately doubled the trouble. If the person remained calm though, when a horse was scared or confused, agreeably showing the horse what to do, and giving it the time to understand, it could settle down and start again.

When Rarey was about ten years old, he put his ideas of steady gentleness to the test with an untrained bay colt that his father gave him. He did all the training himself, and the colt became an excellent riding and trick horse. After this success, people began sending their young horses to him to start under saddle and in harness, even though he was still a boy.

This early shouldering of responsibility that working with horses gave him, was soon to help him hold up to a much heavier burden. In the winter of 1839, after Ravey had turned eleven, his father died on Saturday 2 February, at the age of fifty-three.

His mother was left with the enormous undertaking of keeping everything going, plus dealing with the grief of losing her husband. She decided to close the tavern, and concentrate on the farm. Fortunately, several of her older children were not too far away. Her daughter Margaret, was married to Dr John Jones, and living nearby, raising her own family. Elizabeth had married a man named Fairrington, and was in the vicinity; and William H. and his wife Eliza lived on a farm up the road.

The family was hit again by sadness in the autumn when John's grandmother, Margaret Rarey, passed away on 10 October. The following year though, seemed to be brighter. Rarey was earning money for training horses, and even advertising in the newspaper to do so.

In the meantime, he was also learning something which only twenty per cent of adults of the time could do – to read and write. He went to school at an academy run by the Bishop Washburn, a short distance away in town.

His brother William H., later became instrumental in establishing and naming the town as Groveport. Previously in 1833, Jacob Wirt had leased some land from Adam Rarey alongside the Ohio–Erie Canal. He opened a warehouse and store there, and in 1843, drew plans for a village on the west side of the main street.

The following year, William H. Rarey planned the other half of town lying on the east side. This section became known as Rarey's Port. When Wirt became postmaster, he named the whole town Wirt's Grove; however, many letters came addressed to Rarey's Port. Finally to end the confusion, a public meeting was called. A compromise was reached by dropping both personal names, and the town became Groveport. By 1850, the population of Groveport was 483, and there were three stores – groceries, dry goods, and a drug store; four churches, three doctors and a schoolhouse.

When John Rarey was nineteen, he attended preparatory or high school classes being held at Ohio Wesleyan College in Delaware, Ohio. He must have boarded there during the semesters, for it was too far away to commute, the college being located north of Columbus. He was there for the school year 1847–8, and never returned.

In the autumn of 1850, Rarey joined some friends for an exciting journey to the 'Queen City of the West' – Cincinnati. They were going to see Ohio's first State Fair, held from 2 October to the 5th. People streamed into the city to see the Agricultural, Horticultural, and Mechanic's Fair. The *Cincinnati Inquirer* estimated on 4 October 1850 that there were some 25,000 people on the fairgrounds, and that '...the streets leading thereto were constantly crowded with carriages passing and repassing'. The Horticultural pavilion displayed various shrubbery, fruits and flowers; and the Mechanic's Fair had exhibits of machinery, inventions and rockaway carriages. The Agricultural Fair was the liveliest event, with entries in the various classes of turkeys, geese, chickens, pigs, cattle, oxen, goats, Spanish and French sheep and, happily, many breeds of horses.

Unhappily, the fair drew unsavoury characters as well. The *Cincinnati Inquirer* related on 4 October that: 'The police have been actively engaged this week in arresting and watching the movements of pickpockets. George Brown and Bill Burke, two notorious thieves, are now in limbo, having been caught in their nefarious acts.'

The activities of the week also featured an evening Agricultural Ball, and a speech by the Governor of Indiana, Mr Wright. In his remarks he spoke about a question that was hanging uneasily in the thoughts of many: '...the recent distracted howl of a dissolution of the Union', but he felt that 'such a change could not possibly be brought about'. A lot of people though, were not sure Mr Wright was right.

A group that knew how to seize the opportunity of a ready made audience as well as speech-giving politicians, was the circus men. The Stokes and Co. Circus set up their canvases at the corner of Race and 13th Street. Their show featured someone who would become one of the greatest somersaulting bareback riders of the century, Levi North, performing with his 'dancing horse' Tammany.

There at the fair, Rarey met a man with a unique mind and powerful personality named Denton Offut, who became a curious but painful catalyst to Rarey's career as a horse trainer. Offut was selling a book he'd written, and offering lessons in his method at his farm in Covington, Kentucky. Intrigued, Rarey bought the book, published in 1846 in Kentucky, called *Denton Offut's Method of Gentling Horses, Their Selection, and Curing their Diseases*. Rarey decided to investigate Offut's method, so he crossed the Ohio River and went to his farm in Kentucky. He must have been impressed, for later on, back at home in Ohio, he tried Offut's suggestions with a horse he was training. The horse was not impressed. He kicked out and broke Rarey's leg.

Time and again, Rarey paid with pain for his mistakes. Dr A. Clark, of Lithopolis, Ohio, later mentioned this in a letter of recommendation for Rarey, dated 10 November 1857.

> While but a stripling of a boy he was noted for his fearlessness in handling wild and vicious horses; and sorely did he often pay for his temerity. Three different times that I now recollect, have I been called, as physician to the family, to reduce or assist in reducing fractured or dislocated bones, occasioned by his experiments with intractable or vicious horses...

Rarey kept experimenting though, determined to find a method that would work with all horses; and within the next year or two, the pieces of the puzzle began to fall in place. He discovered a technique which, when done correctly, produced astonishing results. This system worked without fail, no matter how difficult the horse, and his belief that it was truly a beneficial method for horses and horsemen became unshakeable.

He decided to start teaching it to others, using a plan similar to Denton Offut's idea: this being to write a book of instructions, teach lessons, then give the students a book, and have them promise not to teach it to anyone else. As Offut stated in his book: 'Everyone receiving a copy of this publication, must consider himself thereby tacitly pledging his honor not to divulge the Secret of my Management of Horses.'

Rarey wrote a 62-page book entitled, *The Modern Art of Taming Wild Horses*. In the text he outlined his method, and the principles he believed lay behind the horse's natural responses. Along with instructions, he gave rational arguments for the practical sense and humaneness of treating horses with kindness. He also advised readers to look at training from the horse's point of view – something that few people seemed to consider. He wrote:

> if we were placed in the horse's situation, it would be difficult for us to understand the driving of some foreigner, of foreign ways and foreign language. We should always recollect that our ways and language are just as foreign and unknown to the horse as any language in the world is to us, and should try to practise what we could understand were we the horse, endeavoring by some simple means to work on his understanding rather than on the different parts of his body.

During the next few years, Rarey travelled about Ohio, teaching his method to horse dealers and breeders, and also working with problem horses and those with dangerous vices.

In 1855, he had his book copyrighted, and it was registered on 14 September. In the late months of the year, hearing of the great herds of wild horses running free in Texas, he decided to go and see if his system would work as well with the mustangs. He reportedly travelled south with an old steamboat man named Captain Atkinson, who was probably familiar with the river route to Texas. Steamboats shoved off from Cincinnati, and chugged down the Ohio River to where it intersects the mighty Mississippi River in Cairo, Illinois. The riverboats would continue down 'The Big Muddy' as pioneers called the Mississippi, to Louisiana. Travellers would then take an overland stage across to Texas.

Rarey and the Captain may have set down their dusty bags in Austin, Texas, the town established in 1839 by Moses Austin; for the title page of the third edition of Rarey's book reads: '...revised and corrected in Austin, Texas. State Times office 1856'. Texas was a vast open-faced territory of plains and cactus, and a people with ways most unfamiliar to those raised on farms in the mid-west. The roving life of cattle-raising and running mustangs, fashioned an attitude of independence and toughness, but this often led to callous treatment of the animals they depended on. The established ways of catching and training horses were often brutal and bloody.

On a ranch, Rarey tried his method with some of the wild horses the wranglers had captured. He was very encouraged to see that it worked 'like a charm'. He worked for a while as a horse trainer, and offered his lessons, but those willing to pay were few and far between. After a few months, he was back on the road and river to Ohio.

Upon his return, during 1856, he gave his first public exhibition of horse training at the Ohio Stage Company's yard, located at Gay and 5th Street in Columbus. Rarey did little advertising, but a large group of onlookers gathered. He demonstrated his system with two horses. The first was a three-year-old unbroken colt, owned by David Taylor of Truro Township, which required two men to bring him to the horse yard. In the introduction, the colt kept letting fly at Rarey with both hind feet, but Rarey continually dodged him and went back to work. In the space of twenty minutes, Rarey was sitting on the horse's back, holding an open umbrella.

The second horse belonged to Dr Downes of Columbus. The Doctor had bought the horse for making house calls, but the horse was so unruly, he had never been able to drive it. The horse was brought in, and before fifteen minutes had gone by, the horse was quietly following Rarey about, and then stood patiently as Rarey got on his back and proceeded to play a drum.

The success of his exhibition was good for business, but something came up in the next few months that was harder to deal with than rank horses – dishonest people.

A book came out in 1856 called, *The Newly Discovered Process of Bridling, Riding, and Working Unmanageable Wild Colts* by J. J. Stutzman and J. W. McBride, both of Ohio. The problem was, long passages of it were lifted right out of Rarey's book. In disgust, Rarey took legal action. They had their day in court on 10 February 1857.

The case was filed as John S. Rarey vs. J. Wesley McBride, United States Circuit Court. Southern District of Ohio. In the proceedings, Rarey proved the extracts as being taken directly from his work, and won the case. The result was that McBride and Stutzman's book was withdrawn from sale.

In the midst of this rollercoaster year of 1857, as a financial panic was gripping America with stocks falling and many unemployed, Rarey encountered a person who suddenly envisioned a way to make money in these bleak times. He was R. A. Goodenough, a Canadian produce merchant and Secretary of the Corn Exchange, with a business on Front Street in Toronto. While watching Rarey work, he could hear the clink of the coin in Rarey's extraordinary skills in handling horses.

Goodenough had previous connections with the British cavalry in London, and realized that the military may very well be interested in having Rarey teach the cavalrymen his method. He suggested they form a partnership and go to England, where they would stand a better chance of meeting the officials that could further Rarey's career. Rarey agreed, and the plans were set in motion.

As the first step, Goodenough arranged a demonstration to take place on 21 October, before British cavalry officers at the Stanley Barracks, Fort York in Toronto. In attendance were Lt General Sir William Eyre, Commander-in-Chief of Her Majesty Queen Victoria's Forces in Canada; his Aide-de-Camp, Major P. Robertson, and other principal officials.

As Rarey proceeded with his demonstration, everyone was taken aback with his swift success in handling and gentling all the horses brought out. After the performance, Sir William Eyre and several others graciously wrote letters of introduction for him to the Horse Guards in London.

Sir William Eyre wrote: 'Having witnessed Mr Rarey's system of subduing or taming young horses, I have great pleasure in recommending him.'

Major Robertson, in his letter dated 21 October 1857 related:

> I saw a two year old colt broken in by Mr Rarey in about 20 minutes. The animal had never had a halter on, or been previously handled, but in a very short time, Mr Rarey rode him about...I think if this system is introduced and properly carried out in the Army very important and valuable results will be obtained, for by this system the horse may be brought to the most perfect steadiness and obedience, qualities so valuable for military purposes; and at the same time the animal will retain all its natural courage, fostered and improved by the confidence Mr Rarey's system of training inspires.

Now, with the possibility of a favourable reception in London set on more solid ground, Rarey went home to Ohio to get ready for the biggest and most exciting opportunity of his life. He obtained several more letters of introduction from area farmers and horsemen, the one from Dr Clark, and also a recommendation from the Governor of Ohio, Salmon P. Chase.

By mid November Rarey and Goodenough were on board the steamship 'the Arcadia', sailing across the tumultous seas of the Atlantic Ocean. They were at the beginning of a grand and dangerous adventure, going forward to meet some of the finest horsemen and women in the world – in England during the reign of Queen Victoria.

2

ARRIVING IN ENGLAND

*A*FTER almost a fortnight at sea, the Arcadia finally sailed into the Mersey River and docked at Liverpool on 29 November 1857. Soon after, Rarey and Goodenough were on the road to London, where they found lodging and then prepared to carry out their plans. They called upon the Royal Horse Guards with their letters, and the officers there were interested to see what Rarey's new system had to offer.

A horse was chosen to test his method, a notoriously vicious horse whom no one could handle. This horse, iron grey in colour with a dark temper to match, came from a stable in Piccadilly owned by Joseph Anderson. Anderson was thoroughly disgusted with the horse, for he had recently sold it for a handsome price, but was obliged to take it back, as it had become unrideable and dangerous. He apparently held little hope as to its reform, for he told Rarey that he could 'kill the horse if he chose, for he was incorrigible'. Instead, Rarey put up thirty pounds to guarantee the horse would not be hurt.

At Anderson's stable, Rarey went into a loose box with the horse, who reportedly lashed out at once with both hind feet, and 'uttered a kind of savage yell'. Rarey requested that the assembly of cavalrymen, horsemen, and journalists allow him some moments of privacy to preserve the secret of his system; so he was left alone with the horse.

After fifteen minutes everyone was called in, and they were quite shocked to see Rarey lying on the ground next to the horse, his head upon the horse as if on a pillow. The horse raised its head

John S. Rarey (*Illustrated London News* 24 April 1858)

with a puzzled look at Rarey, but there was no expression of fear. Rarey handled all the horse's legs, and next asked the horse to rise. He then rode the horse in a small yard, with the reins left slack on its neck, guiding it by a slight motion of his hands. After a short while, another man got on the horse and it still showed no signs of alarm, even when the man dismounted off the back end, over the horse's tail.

An eye witness wrote for *Sporting Magazine* that 'it was difficult to imagine he could ever have been the obstinate brute too many could speak of' but he was, and Rarey would only reveal that his system was 'firm but mild', and anyone could learn it.

This startling demonstration caused much curiosity, and increased Rarey's circle of supporters, which now included Major-General Sir Richard Airey, and other gentlemen associated with the court, such as Lord Alfred Paget. A fine horseman, Lord Paget had been groom-in-waiting to Queen Victoria at her wedding to

Prince Albert of Saxe-Coburg-Gotha in 1840.

It soon became apparent from the growing interest that a plan was needed to protect Rarey and Goodenough's interests. In the past, it wasn't a problem that people would keep his secret, since his students lived far apart in rural areas. In London though, everything was reported in the newspapers. His technique would quickly become common knowledge, and this would take away his opportunity to be paid for teaching it.

Rarey's new friends decided to introduce him to Richard and Edmund Tattersall, owners of the famous horse auction establishment at Hyde Park Corner, and home of the Jockey Club.

Tattersall's (Sketch by James Souder, from a drawing by Gustave Dore)

Tattersalls immediately saw that Rarey's system could 'benefit the great horse interest of London'. They helped to formulate a plan which required people who wanted to attend Rarey's lessons to sign a subscription list. Once the list reached 500 names, the lessons would begin. Afterwards, the subscribers were to sign an agreement not to reveal Rarey's method.

Goodenough decided that the price for lessons should be ten guineas – equivalent to about 200 pounds today – payable in advance. It was outrageous, but if it worked, it would be Goodenough's pot of gold at the end of Rarey's rainbow. The Tattersalls said they would hold the subscription funds in trust, without any commission paid to them, until the lessons were given. At the Tattersalls request, the treasurer and secretary of the fund was to be Samuel Sidney, an equestrian author and hunting correspondent for the *Illustrated London News.*

An invitation was soon afterwards extended from the Royal Horse Guards, for Rarey to visit Prince Albert's farm, known as Shaw Farm, near Windsor. There, Rarey gave a demonstration before Prince Albert's equerry – the officer in charge of his horses – Colonel Alexander Hood, and his wife Lady Mary Hill, and others. Colonel Hood and his wife were so impressed, that they related what they had seen to the Queen and Prince Albert.

Intrigued by the report, Queen Victoria expressed a wish to see Rarey as soon as possible, and a presentation was arranged to be held at the riding school at Windsor. Prince Albert selected a defiant cream-coloured stallion for the demonstration, and had him sent to the stables there. On Wednesday morning, 13 January 1858, Rarey and Goodenough took the train west from London. After a bouncy journey of twenty-one miles, they arrived in Berkshire, and then rode in a carriage up the long straight road leading to Windsor Castle.

AN AUDIENCE WITH QUEEN VICTORIA

*D*AYLIGHT flowed into the windows of the riding house at Windsor, as Rarey's demonstration was about to begin. Rarey, top hat in hand, was introduced to Her Majesty Queen Victoria, Prince Albert, and members of the Royal family and court. As Rarey went through his presentation, what did the Queen really think about him?

Fortunately, through the expressive hand of Queen Victoria, we have a written record of what she saw and felt on that January afternoon in the following entry in her journal:

> We walked with Vicky and Bertie [Victoria the Princess Royal and the Prince of Wales Edward Albert] and all the Ladies and Gentlemen down to the stables to see the wonderful performance of the 'American Whisperer' on the horse, which is indeed most extraordinary. It is a secret, which he will only impart for a large sum of money. Sir R. Airey, who was there, knows it, and can himself practise on horses, making the most vicious ones do anything, and all with such gentleness. We saw the performance in the Riding School. The first, a colt, was very large and heavy, and would not lie down, as the man wished him to do. He asked us to walk out for twenty minutes, which we did, and by the time we all returned, this raw beast submitted to everything, even to the loudest drumming on, and under him. Mr Anderson's horse did, in six lessons, what no skilled and well broken one at Astley's [a circus] could do. Albert allowed 'Hamir' to be tried, but in the loose box, and for nearly three quarters of an hour, after which Mr Rarey got him down and put his hands between his hind legs! The horse seemed hot but not distressed in any way. This Mr Rarey says that anyone can learn to do, even a child! It is wonderful.

Four days later Rarey wrote a letter to his oldest sister Margaret Rarey Jones, about that exciting day. Sara Lowe Brown, his grand-niece, quoted the letter in her book, *The Horse Cruiser and the Rarey Method of Training Horses*:

17 January 1858

After the Royal Family entered the Riding House, Queen Victoria and Prince Albert came in and to the front, where I was introduced to Her Majesty and the Prince Consort. While sitting on the back of a large wild colt, which stood perfectly quiet with its head up, I, facing the party with my hat in my hand, made a short speech to the Queen. A drum was afterwards handed me which I beat with fury, without the horse exhibiting any signs of fear.

After taming a second horse, the riding master [Mr Meyers] selected a horse belonging to Prince Albert, a wild, nervous animal. I was in a box stall alone with the horse for 15 minutes. When Queen Victoria and Prince Albert entered, they found the animal lying down, and I lying beside him with one of his hind feet under my head and the other over my chest. This so astonished them that they laughed. As the place was not large all could not see, so after the Queen and Prince Consort had looked, they stepped back to let others of the royal party have a look. After that, the Queen and Prince Consort came back, talking to me about the horse, inquiring if I could make him rise. I answered, 'Yes', and commanded the animal to rise to his feet. They stood looking at the horse and said it was a wonderful performance, thanked me for the entertainment and departed.

After the exhibition I was shown through the castle from kitchen to cellar, the state-rooms, and the Queen's private rooms. It was a very interesting sight. I also dined in the castle and, the next day, I received a note by the special command of the Queen, with a cheque enclosed for $125, a gift for my entertainment. She also sent a messenger to know if I would again appear before Her Majesty and the royal guests in attendance for the royal marriage. I accepted the invitation and will have the honor of addressing more royalty, perhaps, than has ever been brought together on any previous occasion.

On this Sunday the 17th, when Rarey was writing his letter, a host of foreign dignitaries was arriving by the hour. Inside the castle, the Royal Family was in an uproar. Queen Victoria and Prince Albert had been on edge for weeks due to the forthcoming marriage on 25 January of their eldest daughter, seventeen-year-old Victoria,

the Princess Royal. She was engaged to marry the twenty-six-year-old Crown Prince of Prussia, Frederick William. Her parents were happy about the union, but after a brief honeymoon at Windsor, she was to go to live with her new husband in Berlin, Germany. The dread of this separation multiplied the normal anxieties of a wedding.

The royalty arriving on the 17th included numerous young princes from Prussia and Germany with their 'ferocious moustaches'. They included: Prince Hohenzollern Sigmaringen; the Count of Flanders (son of King Leopold of Belgium); Prince Julius of Holstein Glucksburg; Prince William of Baden; the Duke of Saxe-Coburg and Gotha (Prince Albert's' birthplace); and other members of the Prince Consort's family and relations.

The need for extra guest rooms rapidly became a sticky problem. Prince Albert solved it by extending an invitation to visit their home in Scotland in the interval before the wedding. The bridegroom, Prince Frederick William, was not scheduled to arrive until Saturday the 23rd, but a steady stream of others did, requiring the necessity of setting dinner places for eighty to ninety at Buckingham Palace in the evening.

The travelling royalty may have been taking extra precautions due to a recent assassination attempt. On 15 January in Paris, as the Emperor Napoleon III and the Empress Eugenie emerged from their carriage at the Opera House at 8:30 pm, a bomb exploded. The force of the blast shattered the carriage, but somehow the Emperor and Empress escaped serious harm. Others didn't. Two soldiers of escort were killed and a civilian was mortally wounded. The total receiving wounds was approximately sixty, including the Comptroller of the Opera, police officers, and two ladies watching from windows.

Napoleon's face was scratched from the bursting of glass, but he and the Empress proceeded in and viewed the opera. Four conspirators were later arrested. The main person behind the plot, Orsini, stated before his execution that he believed Napoleon had proven false to Italy.

Queen Victoria knew the terror of being assailed in public. Several attempts had been made on her life during her reign, one only four months after her marriage in 1840. She did not hide herself behind castle walls, but carried on with public duties. The possible lurking of madmen and fanatics could not suppress her, yet it remained to be seen that a colder darkness could.

Presently, the light was shining as the clamour and excitement of the wedding was coming to a climax. On Saturday afternoon, 23 January, in the Riding House at Buckingham Palace, the spotlight was turned onto horses, and how to get along peacefully with them. In attendance alongside the Royal Family and the guests from European royal houses, was the Princess Royal and her fiancé Prince Frederick William, although he was still quite shaken from a boisterous sea crossing.

John Rarey entered the elegant Riding House attached to the Royal Mews, and stood before his sparkling audience. After his introductory remarks, he stepped aside while Lord Alfred Paget gave a demonstration with a dapple grey pony belonging to the Prince of Wales. This was to show that Rarey's system could be learned and used by others, in contrast to that of Dan Sullivan, the famous 'Horse Whisperer'. Sullivan jealously guarded his secret of how he subdued riotous horses, and would not even tell his sons. The horses he worked with came out calm, but terrified, and quickly returned to former vices when handled by others.

After Lord Paget had finished with the pony, Rarey brought in Anderson's horse, surprising everyone with its performance. The *Illustrated London News* of 30 January 1858 reported that the horse 'lay down at his bidding and followed him like a dog around the building. Placing himself at one end of the riding school, he called to the animal which he had left at the other and it immediately cantered towards him in a playful manner.'

The next horse brought in was Prince Albert's cream-coloured stallion. 'This animal,' the article continued,

> has never permitted anyone to ride him, but he allowed Mr Rarey to mount him without offering the least resistance. With this the exhibition terminated, and the Queen and her illustrious visitors, by whom it was witnessed with the most evident tokens of interest and wonder, took their departure.
>
> The principle on which Mr Rarey goes, is one of extreme kindness and tenderness towards the animal, the object being to convince him that man is his natural master and friend, and to elicit his confidence and kindly regard. Mr Rarey appeals to what he calls, 'the intellect and affections of the horse', and states that this is the secret of all his success.

A marked change was seen in Anderson's horse
(*Harper's Magazine* April 1861)

A flurry of publicity arose from the exhibition at Buckingham Palace, and the follow-up articles in the papers. The front page news however, was the royal wedding. Rarey was assigned a seat at the Chapel Royal, St James Palace on Monday morning, 25 January, when the Princess Royal in silk and lace joined her groom at the altar. The Archbishop of Canterbury performed the service. The vows were mixed up, but so had it been at the Queen's wedding at this same altar. The Queen was the picture of composure, even though in a pre-wedding photo with Prince Albert and the Princess Royal, she trembled so briskly the picture was blurred.

After a brief honeymoon at Windsor, the time came for the couple to depart for Germany. The heartache of parting on that cold cloudy morning of 2 February was keenly felt by all. Several days later, Princess Victoria, still in a swirl of emotion and homesickness, was surprised with a warm reception in Berlin, where she was hailed as 'The Fairest Flower of Albion'.

The Queen and Prince Albert strove to return to a normal routine for the sake of the kingdom and their remaining eight children at home. One light order of business was to have their names placed on Rarey's subscription list at Tattersalls, along with that of the sixteen-year-old Prince of Wales. The subscription list soon blazed with glittering and noble names like the Duke of Wellington, the son of the famous Waterloo general, and an impressive listing of Earls, Marquises, Marchionesses, Dukes and Duchesses; and the 'idol of Yorkshire', the respected horseman Sir Tatton Sykes. Samuel Sidney described Sir Tatton as 'six feet high, all bone and muscle, always on horseback; and perhaps the finest amateur horseman that ever rode a race'.

Another celebrated name was that of Lord Palmerston, the 'rogue elephant of politics', who stood out in a crowd with his vibrant 'waffling laugh' and dyed whiskers. Lord Palmerston enjoyed riding tall horses, and had long held a keen interest in the turf. Several years earlier he'd had a winning three-year-old colt sired by 'Venison' – a descendant of 'the immortal chestnut Eclipse', whose portrait hung over the fireplace at Tattersalls.

In February 1858, although the subscription list had started off grandly, it began to flag at the midpoint of 250 names. For the general public, the cost was a big sticking point, and there was suspicion of fraud due to the very rapid cure of the horse's vices. In the meantime, Rarey and Goodenough decided to open another list in France. Tattersalls offered to let them hold a demonstration at their French headquarters, so the partners travelled across the English Channel to France. At Tattersall's office in Paris, Goodenough arranged to open the new list and send out advertisements, while Rarey started searching for dangerous horses.

When word came to the government breeding farm at Cluny, as to what kind of horses Rarey was looking for, all thoughts turned to Stafford. This dark bay 'half-bred, half-mad coaching stallion' was only six years old but was on the brink of destruction because of his utter disregard for humans. For the last year he had refused to be groomed, or to let anyone in his box, as he greeted them with his mouth open ready for action. If Rarey wanted the worst of horses, the managers at Cluny reasoned, he was going to get it. Stafford was muzzled and sent to Paris.

The showdown with Stafford was set for Monday 8 March. When the day came, Tattersalls arena overflowed with some 300 people: sportsmen, horsemen, members of the Jockey Club, and a commission appointed by Emperor Napoleon III, the nephew of the war commander Napoleon Bonaparte. Stafford was brought in blindfolded and muzzled, thrashing about between two ropes anchored by a pair of frightened attendants. Given the signal to cut the ropes, a third man desperately sawed away at them until finally the ropes gave way and Stafford was free.

The audience, having seen that Stafford was anxious to give Rarey his best shot, was asked to leave. Now, face to face with this horse that had a head 'shaped like a coffin', Rarey set to work. He managed to get close enough to put a hand on Stafford, but then as he was handling the horse's leg, Stafford suddenly whipped around and grabbed Rarey by the shoulder. Shaking him about, he had no intention of letting go, until Goodenough stepped lively and rushed in with a pitchfork. Rarey wasn't hurt badly. He took a few minutes to settle himself, shook off the incident and continued with the job ahead of him.

After a long hour and a half session with Stafford, Rarey rode him into the arena in front of the audience. The *Paris Illustrated Journal* reported that:

> The appearance of the horse was completely altered, he was calm and docile. His docility did not seem to be produced by fear or constraint, but was the result of perfect confidence. The astonishment of the spectators was increased when Mr Rarey unbridled him, and guided the formerly savage animal, with a mere motion of his hands or indications with his leg, as easily as a trained circus horse. Then, dashing into a gallop, he stopped him short with a single word ...
>
> Stafford was afterwards ridden by a groom, and showed the same docility in his hands as in those of Mr Rarey. He succeeded on the first attempt in putting him in harness with a mare, although he had never had his head through a collar before; [he drove them out in the street] and they went as quietly as the best broken carriage horses in Paris.

An English newspaper in Paris, *Galignani's Messenger* on 11 March 1858 added that after driving Stafford:

> He then rode him, and without a bridle turned him in every direction, and ended by firing a five-barrelled revolver off his back. He then rode him into the school, and beat the drum and opened an umbrella repeatedly, and still without a bridle ... A competent man, M. Baucher, who has handled more horses than most people, on signing his name as a subscriber said, 'After having received communication

of Mr Rarey's system, I declare that his system is infallible, of an excellent practical application, and based upon principles the most natural and rational.'

It must have been a thrill for Rarey to meet the horseman, Baucher, for he had studied Baucher's books on horsemanship and had even quoted him in his own book.

Another person favourably impressed was the Emperor Napoleon III, who added his name to the subscription list.

As the news of Stafford's transformation reached England, Rarey's friends in London wrote to him, urging his swift return. The subscribers were anxious for his lessons to begin, and something else had happened while he was away. Something which they knew Rarey could not, should not resist.

4

THE ACID TEST: THE INFAMOUS STALLION CRUISER

*T*HE something was a public dare, published in the *Morning Post* on 2 March 1858. A sporting correspondent who signed his columns 'Argus', threw down the gauntlet with the following challenge:

> Mr Rarey is a public man, and, of course, exposed to criticism. Some of his experiments have been successful, but there has not been enough time to see whether the docility of those horses upon whom he has operated is as durable as he alleges.
>
> If, however, he would 'walk over the course', and set criticism at defiance, let him go down some morning to Murrel's Green with a few of his aristocratic friends, and 'try' Cruiser, and if he can ride him as a hack, I would guarantee him immortality, without a single further advertisement, and an amount of ready money that would make a British bank director's mouth water ...
>
> Cruiser was the property of Lord Dorchester, and was a good favorite for the Derby in Wild Dayrell's year, but broke down about a month before the race. Like all Venison horses [Venison was his sire], his temper was not of the mildest kind, and John Day was delighted to get rid of him. When started for Rawcliffe [a breeding farm near York], he told the man who led him on no account to put him into a stable, as he would never get him out.
>
> This injunction was of course disregarded, for when the man wanted some refreshment, he put him into a country public-house stable, and left him, and, to get him out, the roof of the building had to be pulled off.
>
> At Rawcliffe, he was always exhibited by a groom with a ticket-of-leave bludgeon in his hand, and few were bold enough to venture into

31

Muzzled and miserable (*Harper's Magazine* April 1861)

his yard – the cordial wish of every visitor to the sale apparently being 'that some friendly bullet would lay him low'.

This animal then, whose temper had depreciated him perhaps a thousand pounds in value, I think would be 'the right horse in the right place' for Mr Rarey; and, as the locale is so near to London, the sooner the experiment is made the better for his own interest...

Following the column was a letter from Cruiser's owner, Guy Carleton, Earl of Dorchester, written at his estate, Greywell, located in Hampshire at Murrel's Green. He confirmed the information, adding that Cruiser,

...was bred by me in 1852, and I consider him to have been vicious from a foal; he was always troublesome to handle, and showed temper on every opportunity. On his road here from Danebury, he went on his knees and tore the ground up with his teeth. I have seen him lean against the wall of his box, and kick and scream for ten minutes together.

In 1855 the Rawcliffe Stud Company and myself entered into an agreement respecting him, by which they were enabled to purchase the half of him on reasonable terms, provided they liked his stock; but notwithstanding the latter were much admired, I was requested to remove him after the second season, his savage propensities rendering the care of him too dangerous an office for any man in their employ.

I was assured by the manager of the Rawcliffe Stud that for days he would allow no one to enter his box, and on one occasion tore an iron bar, one inch thick, in two with his teeth. If Mr Rarey can tame him, I feel certain no horse can withstand his art.

As soon as Rarey returned from France, he sent a card to Lord Dorchester – '...requesting particulars concerning Cruiser's character, and that he might be sent to me'.

Dorchester answered saying that Rarey would have to go to the horse, as he was too fierce to be sent. So be it. The next stop for Rarey was the railway station.

'Quietly and as I imagined unknown', Rarey related in a later lecture, as quoted in the 7 January 1861 *New York Times,*

> I went to see the horse. I found the half had not been told – he would bite, kick, beat and throw. No one dared approach him...He would have been killed but his owner hated to lose him as he was a very valuable horse, and of a noted blood breed...
>
> Having kicked to pieces his wooden box, they kept him in a brick one. He was heavily muzzled and strapped and had not been out for two years...The muzzle had almost worn a hole in his head...His sides were bruised, his hips scarified, and there was a wound inside of his knee.
>
> I was compelled to wait until he was healed before I could work on him; so I went back to London, but before I got there, someone had put it in the papers that 'Rarey had been to see Cruiser, and was afraid to touch him.' Under this imputation I remained for three weeks...

Frustrated by the doubts and insults now hanging over his name, Rarey still said nothing to the press. He was content though, with the arrangement he'd made with Lord Dorchester. He would have three months to effect a change for the better in Cruiser, and if successful, he'd receive a one hundred pound bond.

The inevitable backlash of popularity began to mount. Those

on the sidelines eager to pounce on anyone with a new idea, came out in full force. As the proverb from ancient Baghdad proclaimed; 'for every noble horse that neighs, a thousand donkeys set up their discords'.

Veteran horse trainers, understandably envious of Rarey's publicity and financial success, began swinging their battle axes in print. James Telfer of Northumberland staked a claim that he had been using and teaching a similar method before Rarey ever reached the shores of England. He theorized that Rarey learned it from one of his pupils who had gone to America some twenty years before.

Telfer's claims were championed by author Fred Taylor, who had quickly written a book entitled *Telfer's System of Horse Taming*. Telfer gave a public demonstration of his method in London in March, but he had, the papers declared, '...only very partial success'.

Another charge that kept popping up in English and American papers was that Rarey used secret potions or hypnotism to mesmerize horses and achieve his results. It was not out of hand to suspect this, for more than one trainer had tried to hoodwink the public by saying they had special powers over horses, when, in truth, they were using anything from tobacco to sicken horses to the poison strychnine to make them 'safe'. Some trainers put faith in concoctions of scents and oils rubbed on the horse's nose. Others even ground up the chestnuts on horses' legs, and puffed the dust into their horse's nostrils.

Rarey dismissed these charges of 'assistance from the chemist's shop', saying he only used 'the oil of experience'. He had covered this subject in his book, saying:

> The absurdity of trying to break or tame the horse by the means of receipts for articles to smell at, or of medicine to swallow is self-evident...How long do you suppose a horse should have to stand and smell a bottle of oil before he would learn...Although the acts that accompany these efforts – handling him, touching him about the nose and head, and patting him, as they direct you should after administering the articles, may have a very great effect, which they mistake for the effects of the ingredient...

Meanwhile, by the middle of March, Rarey was preparing to begin teaching his lessons, even though the list had still not reached 500 names. The lessons were to consist of an hour and a half lecture,

'...illustrated by one or more horses of a refractory disposition', as his advertising portfolio stated.

On St Patrick's Day, Rarey gave a private demonstration for the Duke of Wellington at his private riding school in Knightsbridge, as a courtesy for being allowed to hold his lessons there. The first official lecture was given on 20 March. The men and ladies who attended signed an autograph sheet; and Lord Palmerston under his signature wrote, 'I have witnessed Mr Rarey's proceeds with great satisfaction.'

The Captain of the Royal Horse Guards, Duncan Baillie agreed with this, for after seeing Rarey's lecture on 25 March at Cumberland Lodge, he sent a letter from the Cavalry Barracks adding that he considered the system; '...very effectual with vicious or unsteady horses and very useful to any one who is in any way connected with horses'.

A man connected with horses of the turf, James Weatherby – the editor and publisher of *The Racing Calendar and Stud Book* – saw a different element in Rarey's work. After attending his class on 31 March, he wrote 'It is a grand thing to teach men to think.'

One man who was thinking of Rarey was the writer Argus. Almost a month had slipped by since his initial suggestion to try Cruiser. Argus decided to renew the challenge in print, publishing a statement about it in the *Morning Post.*

Rarey, stung into action, immediately set off for Murrel Green. Arriving at Greywell on Saturday 3 April, he was greeted by Lord Dorchester. Rarey went out to the stables and at first worked with an untrained two-year-old filly. He then walked with a light step down a small lane – the lane leading to the brick stable of the horse nobody liked.

As Rarey came near Cruiser's stable, the straw rustled, and then came the sound of a loud snort, and the stamp of a foot. It was rather dark inside, but Rarey caught a glance of the white in Cruiser's eye, which shimmered in the dim light. As Lord Dorchester spoke about Cruiser, Rarey stood listening with his arm lying over the open half of the double door. Next, as Rarey told the story during a lecture:

> I opened the door and walked in. Cruiser was astonished at seeing this and more so by my exhibiting no fear. I stood still. He came slowly up to smell of me after a while. When I saw that he would stand, I began to

stroke him. At a sound he started back frightfully. Lord Dorchester begged me to tie his head, and I did so, but then you never saw such fighting. Knowing that he would either kill himself or tear down his box, I released him and began all over again.

Lord Dorchester, fearful for my safety, advised me to go no further, but I had too much confidence in my principles to recede. I did not try to hurt him, but instead to establish confidence between us. I asked Lord Dorchester not to speak or interfere, at least not until he saw me down under Cruiser's feet and he worrying me. After a while when he allowed me to stroke him again, I then took him into the straw-yard and proceeded as with any other horse.

And here is where the secret of Rarey's system came into play. It seemed simple in theory, but the results were dramatic. As Rarey had explained in his book:

> There is something in the operation of taking up one foot that conquers a horse quicker and better than anything else you could do, and without any danger of hurting himself or you either; for you can tie up his foot and sit down and look at him until he gives up...there is a principle of this kind in the nature of the horse, that by conquering one member, you conquer to a great extent, the whole horse.

After hobbling the fore leg with a simple strap, Rarey used another strap and a surcingle to manoeuvre the horse in a series of steps to lie down. The second part of his method was critically important, and it happened after the horse was on the ground.

The steps of Rarey's method. Step 1 – the leg strapped up
(*Rarey's Art of Taming Horses*; drawings said to be of Cruiser)

Straps 1 and 2 in place (*Rarey's Art of Taming Horses*)

Rarey stroked, soothed, gentled and spoke very quietly to the horse. In the book he detailed the process saying: 'Take off the straps and straighten out his legs; and rub him lightly about the face and neck with your hand the way the hair lies, handle all his legs and after he has lain a few minutes, let him get up again.'

Samuel Sidney, who witnessed Rarey working with horses many times related in a later edition of Rarey's book, that when the horse was lying down,

> every limb must be gentled…In moving round him for the purpose of gentling him, walk slowly always from the head around the tail and again to the head…caress and rub his ears…scrape the sweat off him with a scraper, smooth the hairs of his legs and draw the fore one straight out…the leg first strapped being hand-rubbed to restore circulation, other wise a horse is likely to stumble with the benumbed limb…You must now go over him again as if you were a mesmeric doctor or shampooer, with the caresses that horses evidently like. It is by this continual soothing and handling that you establish confidence between yourself and the horse…like every other operation, it must be done very gently, and accompanied by soothing words.

Rarey advised in his text:

> Always follow each touch or communication of this kind with the most tender and affectionate caresses, accompanied with a kind look, and pleasant word of some sort, such as, 'Ho! my little boy – Pretty boy!'

'Nice lady!' or something of that kind, constantly, repeating the same words, with the same kind, steady tone of voice; for the horse soon learns to read the expression of the face and voice, and will know as well when fear, love, or anger prevails, as you know your own feelings; two of which, FEAR and ANGER, A GOOD HORSEMAN SHOULD NEVER FEEL.

Rarey apparently did not feel any fear with dangerous horses, but he knew it took firmness, as well as patience, to handle a horse that held no fear of man. But how could anyone safely get a strap on the foreleg of a horse like Cruiser? Rarey solved this by having a big wagon brought in 'that would have served for a barricade in a revolution', and had it filled with hay. Rarey positioned himself under the wagon, behind one of the wheels and waited. Eventually when Cruiser overcame his suspicion and ventured to nibble some hay, Rarey reached through the wheel and fastened the strap.

Horse struggling (*Rarey's Art of Taming Horses*)

A struggle ensued but Rarey persisted, not fighting against Cruiser, just following him about, letting him tire himself out. When Cruiser finally lay down, he also placed hobbles on his hind legs, which he didn't normally do, to prevent kicking mischief. In three hours time, Cruiser agreed to be agreeable.

Tiring and going down (*Rarey's Art of Taming Horses*)

Rarey sent for Dorchester to see the results and then put a saddle on Cruiser – the first saddle he'd had on for three years. As Dorchester looked on, Rarey trotted Cruiser up and down the lane, and then asked Dorchester if he'd like to try him. And he did.

In the afternoon, Rarey set off for London, driving a horse hitched to a two-wheeled 'dog' cart with Cruiser tied to the back. Cruiser was no doubt quite puzzled by everything that was happening to him. They travelled about forty miles, stopping for the night at a place called Virginia Water.

Samuel Sidney, in an edition of Rarey's book that he edited, *The Art of Taming Horses*, wrote that Rarey

> did not lose a moment but set to work the same night to tame him – limb by limb, and inch by inch…first rendering him helpless by a gag-bit, straps and hobbles, then caressing him, then having him lie down, then caressing him again, stoking every limb, talking to him in soothing tones, and now and then if he turned vicious, taking up his helpless head, giving it a good shake, while scolding him as you would a naughty boy. And then again taking off the gag and rewarding him with a lock of hay and a drink of water, then making him rise and riding him, making him stop at a word…The most curious and important fact of

all in connection with this strapping up and laying down process, is, that the moment the horse rises, he seems to have contracted a personal friendship for the operator, and with a very little encouragement will generally follow him around.

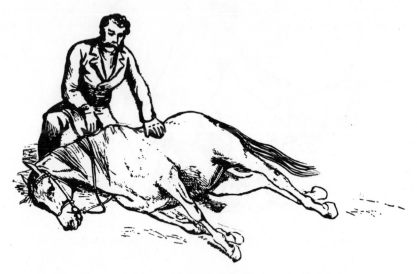

Final step – soothing and stroking (*Rarey's Art of Taming Horses*)

Would this affection ever spring forth in a horse as embittered against mankind as Cruiser? The test would come when Rarey and Cruiser met the public in London.

5

CRUISER MEETS THE PUBLIC

*C*RUISER'S arrival in London on Sunday, quietly trotting behind Rarey's cart, created a storm of sensation. Like Daniel, Rarey had emerged from the den on friendly terms with the lion. There was a strange power at work here, and everyone was eager to hear the secret.

In the *Morning Post*, a new letter from Lord Dorchester appeared dated 7 April, verifying everything that had happened at Greywell. People shook their heads in wonder.

Riding the crest of the wave, a special lecture featuring Cruiser was announced for Saturday 10 April. The ailing subscription list suddenly swelled with names and filled to overflowing. All were anxious to see Cruiser take the stage, this horse whose temper could 'tower into a frenzy'. Due to the demand, the site for lessons was moved to the riding school at the Round House on Kinnerton Street in Belgravia.

The newspapers stirred up such interest that Cruiser's first public appearance became a social event. This was helped along by Goodenough placing in the advertisements, 'subscribers may bring ladies by the payment of an extra five guineas'.

On Saturday 10 April, 'Mr Rarey's Cruiser Soiree', as *Sporting Magazine* called it, was about to begin. A soiree was a party without dancing, and this lecture had definitely taken on the atmosphere of a party. Samuel Sidney, secretary of the subscription list, was there and described the scene in Rarey's book:

> long before the doors were open, the little back street was filled with a fashionable mob, including ladies of the highest rank...A hatful of ten

Mr Rarey's Cruiser soiree – Cruiser's first appearance in London, drawn by John Leech

guinea subscriptions was thrust upon the unwilling secretary at the door, with as much eagerness as if he had been an allotter of shares in a ten per cent railway...and it must be observed that this crowd included among the mere fashion-mongers, almost every distinguished horse-man and hunting man in the three kingdoms.

At the appointed hour, excitement was crackling in the air as Rarey appeared before the crowd. After a few remarks, he plunged into the story of his meeting with 'the most vicious horse I ever saw'. Finally he broke the suspense and announced the star of the show – Cruiser.

'Instead of a blood thirsty savage', wrote *Sporting Magazine* in the May 1858 issue

a mild, plain-looking animal came trotting in as gentle as a foal...He went at once to one corner and put his nose up to the visitors to be patted...His head is long and tapering with a little white on the nose, but there is nothing fierce in his look...Cruiser's hocks are sadly capped from kicking and he stands rather over in one knee...He is aged looking for six years old...'

Mr Rarey said, 'Cruiser shake hands', and he did so, most gracefully lifting his right leg. He then followed Rarey round and round without a rein, stood still when he was told, and came to him when called. He wound up carrying Rarey's cap in his mouth – that mouth which is said to have bitten in twain an iron bar and to have broken a man's arm.

Rarey continued his lecture saying, 'I don't bring Cruiser here to show as a tamed horse and to do all manner of tricks, only to show what a gentle creature he has now become, and that instead of rushing at you to strike you, he will even give you his foot at command.'

A reporter for the *Illustrated London News* wrote on 17 April that Rarey also brought out the relic from Cruiser's dark ages, his iron and leather muzzle:

It was touching to see him look at his old muzzle, which was placed on him to show what he had been – his glance was almost reproachful as if to say 'I am sure I am doing the best I can'.

It was a good day for the English horse when Mr Rarey took ship. The best of the case is the utter absence of all quackery and the plain common sense principle on which the treatment is founded – the theory of gentleness and mutual confidence...Now let us leave off 'breaking' horses, and teach them instead.

The following week from Monday 12 April through Thursday 15 April, Cruiser continued to play the starring role at the Round House. The morning sessions were thoroughly crammed with some 200 people. In the evenings Rarey held private lessons at which 'a couple of Dukes could be seen entering'.

Cruiser's most distinguished visitor was Her Majesty Queen Victoria and several of her children. They stroked Cruiser's soft face and the Queen expressed her sympathy for the hard times Cruiser had been through. There was a record in Prince Albert's account book of £21 paid to Rarey on 14 April, so perhaps the Prince of Wales took a private lesson, or maybe it was for Rarey taking Cruiser to see the Royal Family at the riding school of Buckingham Palace.

On Friday 16 April, Rarey said goodbye to Cruiser and travelled north for two lectures scheduled in Yorkshire for Saturday 17 April and Tuesday the 20th. His next destination was the Emerald Isle. The papers reported that his exhibitions '…excited as much curiosity and interest in Ireland as here'. In Dublin he gave four demonstrations from Monday to Thursday of the week 26 April to the 29th. The lecture on Tuesday was held at The Castle Riding School before the Marquis of Waterford and a select party of ladies and gentlemen.

By May Day, Rarey was back in the busy streets of London, and his first stop was probably the stables at Kinnerton Street. The *Illustrated London News* commented that he 'found Cruiser after their two-week separation in good form and as cordial as ever.'

He resumed his lectures at the Round House, beginning the third of May, and it was elbow to elbow for everyone on those warm spring mornings. At one of the classes, Rarey brought out some 'very cruel spiked bits', to speak against their use.

On 3 May, Rarey had reached the milestone of having taught the original 500 people on the list. The management of the funds was then transferred from Tattersalls to Rarey's partner, Goodenough. Rarey retained an office there at Hyde Park Corner, to handle business matters and the volume of mail he received. One person recalled that it took two secretaries to open all his mail.

A few days later on 6 May, Rarey met another determinedly aggressive horse, almost in the class of Cruiser, known as Mr Gurney's Gray. This grey thoroughbred had objected to all attempts to train him, 'tearing off saddle flaps with his teeth and bursting his girths', and had been dangerous to work with since the tender age of three months old.

After a trying struggle during the lecture, Rarey at last got the straps on and the horse down. The *Illustrated London News* related on 8 May that later on the horse finally 'bore a saddle and let Rarey get on, but showed a disinclination to move'.

Rarey knew that the colt would probably explode if he forced him to go on, so he decided to start all over again. Except something was wrong. Eye-witnesses said that, 'Mr Rarey was evidently very ill and exhausted to what he usually is, and too unwell to have handled the gray.' So, at the request of spectators he took a seat on the sidelines. Here something happened which planted a serious seed of discontent between Rarey and Goodenough. The incident was described by Samuel Sidney in the Rarey book.

> When Mr Rarey was so ill that he was unable to sit Mr Gurney's gray colt, the boasting Mr Goodenough tried his hand, and was beaten pale and trembling out of the circus by that equine tiger; but Mr Thomas Rice, who had had the charge of Cruiser in Mr Rarey's absence up to that time, although he had never before tried his hand at Rareyfying a horse, stuck to the gray colt, and laid him down...[but the next day]...Mr Goodenough claimed the benefit of the victory.

That did not sit too well with Rarey or anyone else.

The following week Rarey must have been feeling up to par, for he gave lessons at the Round House from 10 May to the 13th, and then went off to Paris. He returned about a week later and resumed his lectures.

His popularity with the public soared higher with each passing day. *The Rarey Waltz*, written by Matilda Langen, was played at a state ball held at Buckingham Palace.

The Cruiser connection and the excitement of their demonstrations, kept their names in the newspapers. Rarey even became a favoured target in the clever tongue-in-cheek columns and cartoons of the newspaper *Punch*. One editorial could not resist asking whether Rarey's power could extend to a hippopotamus, since this was essentially a river horse.

It was clear that the editor of *Punch*, Mark Lemon – 'a roly-poly man, sensitive to pathos' – agreed with Rarey's promotion of 'rational and kindly treatment of horses'. For on 15 May, Lemon

Our dear old friend Briggs—having taken the Receipt for Horse-Taming from the Papers—tries some Experiments upon an Animal that he has picked up a Bargain!

Punch 27 March 1858

published the following poem in *Punch* titled 'The Brute Tamer – An Old Song in a New Shape.'

> Had I to tame a vicious Horse,
> Think ye that I would use brute force?
> On no! I should adopt the course of Mr Rarey.
>
> I chanced this morn, a Groom to view,
> In vain attempting to subdue
> A noble but unruly steed;
> He treated him very ill indeed.
> And whilst the animal he smote,
> Used language much too strong to quote:
> At length – I caught him by the throat –
> And exclaimed, Wretch!
> Suppose that is a vicious horse,
> To tame him should'st thou use brute force?
> Nay, nay; thou should'st adopt the course of Mr Rarey.
>
> The groom and I contending thus,
> The populace surrounded us,
> No doubt they hoped that we should fight,
> For their diversion and delight,
>
> But they did not enjoy that wished-for sight,
>
> For thus I appealed to them – 'Good People!'
> Would you to tame a vicious horse,
> Resort to vulgar physical force?
> No! to the plan you'd have recourse
> Of Mr Rarey…'

Mark Lemon, who was also a playwright, and John Leech, one of his principal artists on the staff of *Punch*, both eventually became personal friends of Rarey.

But with the high points came the lows – people who saw fit to attack him in the press. Some writers wrote with their claws out, dropping comments in their columns about the 'transatlantic horse-tamer' who had the 'tact of charming men as well as horses'.

His work was also scorned as being 'effeminate', and only suitable for 'young drawing room ladies, antiquated dowagers, and gentlemen in peg-tops'. Rarey welcomed women to his lectures, despite the shower of harrumphs from men who didn't think women had any business training horses. Rarey believed otherwise, and was later quoted as saying, 'Ladies were my best pupils.' Samuel Sidney agreed, writing in the Rarey book: 'Several ladies have succeeded famously in horse-taming; but they have been ladies accustomed to horses and to exercise.'

Rarey's financial returns brought criticism upon his head, as if he were stealing the money. The fact of his growing bank account unleased a flood of imitators, '…emulating the success of the horse-tamer from Yankee-land'. People were eager to cash in on the high tide of the horse training business. There was even an advertisement in the paper claiming that the grandson of the Horse Whisperer Dan Sullivan was teaching classes in his grandfather's art, even though Sullivan never taught it to anyone!

Back in America, the same phenomenon was occurring, for in the classified section of the *New York Times*, Caleb Rany of New York ran an ad: 'Rarey's Art of Training Horses – the subscriber is engaged in giving instructions in the above valuable art, no drugs used, satisfaction guaranteed.'

Rarey was guaranteed to get a headache from these underhanded attempts at fraud. He had expected resistance to his system, but this type of deceit surprised and depressed him.

Another test of fire was the claim by Mr Cooke of Astley's, the famous circus establishment on Westminster Bridge Road, that he could teach Rarey's secret system, without ever having to part with ten guineas for a lesson. The *Illustrated London News* on 1 May had mentioned that

> Mr Cooke has undertaken to illustrate Mr Rarey's system and exhibit his own skill in horse taming with decided effect. He straps up the foreleg which he ties to a string passed over the back of the animal. He employs a series of jerks until at length the horse falls to the ground exhausted. Mr Rarey has written a letter to the public journal [*The Times*] disclaiming the connection.

Rarey finally responded to the challengers by offering one thousand guineas to anyone who could convince the Tattersalls that they could practise Rarey's method without having taken a lesson. The carrot dangling, a host of trainers gave it their best effort, but the reward money stayed in the bank.

Meanwhile for Cruiser, life with Rarey was agreeing with him. The formerly battle-scarred stallion was rapidly improving in appearance. 'Gradually', the *Illustrated London News* commented, the rough haggard body grew plump and attractive; his eye gleamed with a tranquil Christian brightness instead of the malignant flash that was wont to extinguish grooms and stable boys. His coat assumed a silky smoothness, showing that his old prejudices against the currycomb had passed away...

Another thing that had changed was his owner. Lord Dorchester had generously given Rarey his share of the fifty per cent interest he held in Cruiser; then Rarey purchased the other half from Rawcliffe Stock Company. The mention of Rawcliffe may have brought out the dark side of Cruiser for soon he was to have another adventure, in which he made people jump, just as in the old days.

In the spring, the Howe and Cushing Great American Circus had roared into town with a spectacular street parade through Regent's Park, featuring a forty-horse hitch of matched cream-coloured horses. The circus included such equestrian performers as: Black Eagle the American Trick Horse; the Educated Comic Mules Pete and Barney, James Robinson on a 'Naked Horse', and a troupe of Bedouin Arabs on their beautiful Arabian horses. They certainly brightened the nights in London at the Royal Alhambra Palace in Leicester Square.

One evening their programme listed a new equestrian attraction – Cruiser. Rarey had agreed to allow Cruiser to be exhibited at the circus, to help them enjoy a good night at the box office, and also to see how Cruiser would work with someone else handling the rein.

During the show, the ringmaster, Mr Cooke, introduced Cruiser, who walked serenely into the ring beside a groom. Cooke told of the stallion's lively background, then attempted to demonstrate how he was tamed. He fumbled with the strap, being nervous, and failed time and again to get it buckled. Cruiser became uneasy and then impatient, and soon changed his mind about standing still. In a fit of frustration, tinged with embarrassment, the ringmaster gave Cruiser a snap with the whip. That was a big mistake.

As Samuel Sidney related in Rarey's book, 'Cruiser rushed at his tormentor with such ferocity that he cleared the ring of all the spangled troupe.'

Sara Lowe Brown, in her book *The Horse Cruiser* wrote:

the terrified ring master turned and fled from the ring with his assistant. Cruiser then had the freedom of the premises and leaped from one

Cruiser on the rampage (*Harper's New Monthly Magazine* April 1861)

side of the ring to the other in a high state of excitement. A panic seized the audience, for there was only a low barrier for their protection. They rushed over the backs of the seats towards the exits…Up to this time, Mr Rarey, who had gone to the circus to see how Cruiser would behave himself, had sat calmly looking on; but when matters got to their worst, he left his seat and went down into the ring.

The crowd paused to see the result. Mr Rarey stood as still as a statue holding up his hand and calling 'Cruiser! Cruiser!' The horse looked uneasily at the motionless figure, but, soon approached slowly. Mr Rarey let him approach and when he was quite near, went to him stroking him softly on the face.

As Samuel Sidney remarked, 'from this we learn that such a horse won't be bullied and must not be feared'. The night at the circus proved that Cruiser's spirit had certainly not been snuffed out by Rarey's handling; yet there were still a few kinks to work on.

6

IF HORSES WERE TIGERS

*I*N THE second half of May, Rarey's next and most curious challenger came wearing stripes. Intrigued by a fierce zebra at the London Zoo in Regent's Park, Rarey asked if he'd be allowed to work with him. The zebra keepers probably thought he was crazy or suicidal or both. Witnesses said that when anyone came into the zebra's enclosure, the equine acrobat would 'spring to the top of the hay rack, seize the cross-beam with his teeth and absolutely hang in that position; which extraordinary proceeding enabled him to keep all his feet freely kicking in the air, ready to destroy anyone who should approach him'.

Zebras have long been famed for being feisty fighters. Living among lions who desire them for lunch, zebras are equipped to defend themselves. They do not bluff, they will kick to kill. In Africa, a man who had murdered a zebra foal was later found dead, having been trampled by the whole herd, according to the South African artist, Charles Astley Maberly.

Rarey was apparently ready to face this kind of deadly fury, for the small but mighty horse tiger was shipped to him in a crate 'strong enough to confine three lions'. Samuel Sidney observed that the zebra 'was as savage a kicker as Cruiser, and could kick from one leg as fiercely as others can from two'.

The sketches and descriptions of this zebra as having a rich cinnamon and deep black coat suggest that he was a common zebra (*equus burchelli*). This type, from eastern and southern Africa, has light brown shadows between the black stripes.

In preparation for being alone in the arena with this thirteen-hand dynamo, Rarey tried to think of something to keep the zebra from grabbing his arm or leg. He decided to put a large wooden bit on him – but how, when it was a tricky job just to get near him? Rarey worked out that the best way was to toss a rope around the zebra's neck and then draw him to the bars of the cage. This plan worked, and with nimble fingers he managed to get the bit and bridle on.

At the first lesson, the zebra was brought in, 'firmly lashed and held by his keepers', wrote T. B. Thorpe, in an article for *Harper's New Monthly Magazine*, April 1861. 'While thus restrained, he crunched upon his immense hard wooden bit, screamed like an infuriated hyena [zebra's voices can sound like barking dogs] and flung his heels wildly about, as if desirous of demolishing innumerable keepers' heads.'

At one point, the zebra tucked his head to the side and turned four or five somersaults in a row. The sight amused Rarey, for the paper *Household Words*, edited by Charles Dickens, said that the zebra, 'was the only animal in England that ever made Mr Rarey laugh heartily'.

He needed a good laugh for, after spending four hours with the zebra, he said that it had 'given him more trouble and anxiety than

The zebra (*Rarey's Art of Taming Horses*)

would 400 horses'. Several lessons later, the scrappy little stallion in stripes was still giving him a lot of trouble, but Rarey believed he was ready to meet a bigger audience.

At the Round House on Monday 24 May, a crowd of curious horsemen, humane officers, and writers – Mr William Thackeray among them – came to see what Rarey had up his sleeve with this zebra business. An article in *The London News*, reprinted in the *New York Times* on 10 June, detailed the lively scene saying:

> When at first we heard that Mr Rarey was going to introduce a zebra to his pupils, we had a shrewd suspicion that something like a theatrical coup was contemplated, and some 'wooly horse' who had perhaps graduated in a circus, was about to be introduced for the sake of novelty and attraction. But all suspicion of this sort was dispelled when we saw this wild ferocious animal, so beautiful and yet so terrible, in his beauty, follow the great horse-tamer reluctantly into the ring.
>
> There was something positively unearthly in the scream with which he saluted the company…and he kept up a low whining soliloquy which a person acquainted with the Houynhmn language [the language of the wise horses in *Gulliver's Travels* by Jonathan Swift] might no doubt have translated, 'It would give me intense gratification to devour this fellow where he stands, and to kick out the brains of these impertinent lookers-on immediately afterwards, but unfortunately, there is no justice to zebras now-a-days, so I have nothing for it but to lie quiet, and behave myself henceforth and forever like a civilized quadruped and gentleman…'
>
> He retired slowly and with dignity, rather sad – more than sulky in his deportment, and gave only one flying scream as he passed through his stable door, had one gentle nip at the groom who held it open for him and subsequently permitted a lady of distinction who was present to stroke him…

The zebra had made it clear he was not too thrilled with parading before the public. Rarey didn't do anything more with him right away, for he was leaving for a lecture tour of Manchester, Liverpool, and Scotland. Later though, he exhibited the zebra for the Queen, Prince Albert, and the Royal Family.

During the first week of June, Rarey was a guest at Dunkeld, an estate in Scotland owned by the Duke and Duchess of Athol. Queen Victoria and Prince Albert often enjoyed peaceful holidays there, walking and riding on the thousands of beautiful acres along the river Tay. While the warmth of early summer spread the wildflowers over the countryside, Rarey travelled farther afield. The journeys were tiring but fascinating: on and off steamships, trains, coaches, and there were always new horses to see. Days came and went, visiting palaces, ancient castles, old cramped cities and inns of every size and shape. And Rarey always hoped that they would serve the meals he liked the best: 'Hearty American breakfasts, fish in every shape, and roast potatoes were his delight', as the writer Henry Hall Dixon later observed in *Sporting Magazine.*

In July, his stay in Paris was interrupted by the very unsettling news that his book, *The Modern Art of Taming Wild Horses*, had been published in London without his knowledge. The public was outraged and angry editorials stormed about this '...three penny book tossed into the arena...' For after charging his subscribers such a high rate and then pledging them to secrecy, now a book was suddenly available which described the whole process for anyone to learn. Someone had certainly stabbed him in the back.

Returning at once to London, he released his subscribers from their secrecy pledge through a letter published in *The Times*. Grumblings had been heard earlier about the secrecy issue, for it was difficult for subscribers to find a private place to use Rarey's method with their horses. Only the wealthiest people had their own riding school in which to work without bystanders. So, the time had come to do away with the pledge, but it was an embarrassing way for it to happen. His reputation was tarnished and as J. H. Walsh wrote in his book, *The Horse in the Stable and the Field*, about the appearance of Rarey's book: '...it prevented the payment of any more ten-guinea subscriptions and reduced the charge for the sight of the process to a guinea, and half guinea tickets for seats at the Alhambra'.

People like Walsh who resented his wealth and popularity now had a bigger bandwagon to jump on and hurl insults. Others, though, like the thirty-six-year-old Henry Hall Dixon, an author and contributor to the 'Omni-bus' column of *Sporting Magazine* and various periodicals, stuck by him. Dixon later wrote in *Sporting Magazine*: 'Some few said it was a swindle, but the great majority of the ten-guinea men were so amused with the effrontery of the senior partner [Goodenough] and the uneffected manners of the real actor; as well as his brilliant handling of horses, that they never complained, and quietly took it out by attending nearly every exhibition he had at the Round House and elsewhere and 'had plenty of fun for our money'.

Rarey's steadfast friend, Samuel Sidney, decided to help smooth out the sticky situation by working on a new illustrated edition of Rarey's book. Besides the original text, he planned to include 'the information I have derived from hearing his lectures and seeing his operations on Cruiser and other horses'. Sidney wanted to include enough detail to ensure that people would not hurt their horses or themselves when experimenting with the method. For already, people had received dislocated arms, black eyes, and horses had suffered broken knees. The book was published later in the year by Routledge, with the title, *J. S. Rarey's Art of Taming Horses.*

In July, Rarey's name appeared in print again, but this time the writer wasn't attacking but honestly asking for advice. A letter from 'A Cab-Master' at St James Street Cab-Stand appeared in *The Times* on 23 July inquiring;

> Having read your book about taming of horses to my fellows here, they wish me to beg of you to publish in *The Times* for our benefit and others; your opinion as to whether the blinkers, or winkers as some call them, be necessary for the bridles in harness or not.
>
> We think not, because we see cart and cab horses going without them, and we know they do hurt our horse's eyes this hot dusty weather; moreover, it always seems to us that horses always look more frightened when they hear a noise and can't see what's-a-coming behind them. Otherwise, your opinion will help settle the point for us. And we are obliged by your lessons of humanity already.
>
> I am, Sir,
>
> A CAB-MASTER

Rarey's lengthy reply, published in *The Times* on 28 July, reveals not only his ideas about blinkers, but his depth of understanding and appreciation of horses.

> To the Editor of *The Times*
> Sir,
> Having been requested in the accompanying letter to give my opinion in regard to the use of blinkers on horses through the medium of your valued paper, for the benefit of the cabmen of London, and believing it to be a subject in which the general public are interested, I take great pleasure in stating that all my experience with, and observation of, horses, proves clearly to me that blinkers should not be used and that the sight of the horse, for many reasons, should not be interfered with in any way.

Horses are only fearful of objects which they do not understand or are not familiar with, and the eye is one of the principal mediums by which this understanding and this familiarity are brought about.

The horse, on account of his very amiable nature, can be made in the course of time to bear almost anything in any shape, but there is a quicker process of reaching his intelligence than that of wearing it into him through his skin and bones; and he, however wild or nervous, can be taught in a very short time to understand and not to fear any object, however frightful in appearance.

Horses can be broken in less time and better without blinkers; but horses that have always worn them will notice the sudden change and must be treated carefully the first drive. After that they will drive better without the blinkers than with. I have proved by my own experiments that a horse broken without blinkers can be driven past any omni-bus, cab, or carriage on a parallel with him as close as it is possible for him to go, without ever wavering or showing any disposition to dodge. I have not, in the last eight or ten years constantly handling horses, both wild and nervous, ever put blinkers on any of them, and in no case have I ever had one that was afraid of the carriage he drew behind him or of those he passed in the streets.

The horse's eye is the life and beauty of the animal as well as the index of his emotions. It tells the driver, in the most impressive character, what the horse's feelings are. By it he can tell the first approach of fear in time to meet any difficulty; he can tell if he is happy or sad, hungry or weary. The horse too, when permitted to see, uses his eyes with great judgment. He sees better than we do. He can measure distance with his eyes better than we can, and if allowed free use of them, would often save himself by the quickness of his sight from collisions when the driver would fail to do so by a timely pull on the reins. It would also save many accidents to pedestrians in the streets, as no horse will run onto any person that he can see...

I have yet to find the man who, having once left them off, can be persuaded to put them on again. They are unnecessary and an injurious encumbrance to the horse, and I feel confident, if the cabmen of London will leave them off one year, that blinkers on cab-horses will never be seen again in the streets, and will only be a thing to be read of as one of the follies happily reformed in the 19th century.

I am, Sir, your obedient servant,

J. S. Rarey

However, as Rarey was learning, the most difficult animals to reform were those in human skins; for his suspicions about someone close to him were becoming too strong to ignore.

7

LANDS OF ICE AND FURY

*A*S JULY melted into August in 1858, Rarey and Goodenough dissolved their partnership. The question of who was behind the fiasco of Rarey's book being released in London was never publicly answered, but more than one person pointed in the direction of Goodenough. As a manager he was shrewd and daring, but his loud personality and 'sharp-fisted' dealings did not endear him to anyone. Goodenough, in a huff, booked a passage on a steamer to North America.

The summer of 1858, even though it was known as the summer of the 'great stink' because of the overpowering scent of the Thames, was not all bad for Rarey. One evening as a guest at the Garrick Club, he had the honour of meeting Mr Charles Dickens. Dickens had suffered some trying months as well, with the public announcement during June in *Household Words* of the separation from his wife Catherine. He was climbing steadily back to favour however, by giving public readings of his novels at St Martin's Hall.

The *Illustrated London News* noted that 'Mr Charles Dickens is an excellent reader. He uses little action, but he can make his features eloquent...he impersonates the different characters of his stories, and brings them ideally, but vividly, before the spectator's mind.'

Rarey was looking ahead to the days of autumn and another journey. Encouraged by the invitations he'd received, he decided to tour some of the major capitals of the Continent. The connections between continents was on everyone's mind in August, for on the 17th the first message was received via the transatlantic cable running under the ocean from London to New York. This

Mr Charles Dickens (*Illustrated London News* 1858)

link-up between two worlds gave rise to great rejoicing on both sides of the ocean. Grand jubilees with ringing bells, fireworks, and the crack of gun salutes celebrated the triumphant news.

At the beginning of September, Rarey carried his bags on to a ship bound for Stockholm, Sweden. *Sporting Magazine*, mentioned his itinerary, noting he was 'accompanied by Mr Robson, a Boston friend'.

By mid September, their ship was still steaming to Sweden. Rarey jotted down in his journal for Thursday 23 September: 'This morning at 8 o'clock, we reached the town of Ranea [possibly Ronne on the Danish island Bornholm or Ronneby on the coast of Sweden]. Our steamer was the first that ever went into this port, and the people from the village about three miles distant, rushed out to see the boat come in.'

When they reached Stockholm, Rarey was invited by the Prince Regent, who was later crowned King, to give a presentation at the Royal Riding School. At the demonstration, attended by some 200 people, the Prince Regent remarked that he had been following the accounts of Rarey's horse-training in the newspapers, and had selected an untrained four-year-old Anglo-Arab for him to grapple with.

At one point during the show, the Royal Family jumped to their feet in excitement while watching Rarey with the horses. The Prince Regent afterwards questioned him about different points of training. Then, as a mark of esteem, the Prince presented him with a medal, which would entitle him to special privileges in the kingdom.

During his ten-day stay in Stockholm, Rarey gave several more lectures. There, he wrote the following in his journal on 8 October, which Sara Lowe Brown included in *The Horse Cruiser*.

This morning while looking for vicious horses for my class, I went to the horse butcher's in Stockholm, where I saw one of the most disgusting sights I ever witnessed in my life. On entering the building I saw the carcasses of lately killed horses strewn about the building, hind and fore quarters against the wall, with many bones that had been stripped of flesh scattered around on the floor. Meat ground up like sausage was lying in heaps on benches. In the next room were the heads of three horses that had just been killed, furnishing the supply of meat just referred to. The heads were skinned, all except the tip of the nose which, together with the sunken eyes and tongue hanging out from between the teeth, made a ghastly sight to look at.

I contrasted this with the description of Job's mighty war steed and the description of the horse by Byron and other poets, and my own experience with horses on the western prairies where I had seen one troop of 600 gallantly following their leader, making the earth tremble beneath their tread as they passed like a flying cloud, the sound of their hoofs like distant thunder.

I have always placed the horse next to man in courage, spirit, and ambition, and with the cruel spectacle before me, I could only think of the cannibals of the South-Sea Islands and compare the eaters of this noble animal as little better than those inhuman characters of the human family who, like the vilest of the brute creation, eat each other.

Just outside of the building stood two more of those patient servants of man ready for the sacrifice. It was easy to see at a glance that age and great labor had robbed them of that spirit and strength which could make them of longer use to their masters; and that they were destined for the slaughter with the same philosophy that the heathen choose the aged and helpless of their own species for their meat. These persons are worse than the heathen because they live in an enlightened country.

I shall never forget the appearance of the poor animals and the thoughts and impressions made on my mind at that moment. One had been a gray but was now on account of age almost white, with thin mane, sway back, and broken knees; the other, a sorrel equally thin and aged, showing prominently its ribs and hip bones. They had just arrived from a long distance in the country, for they bore the marks of late rapid travelling. Their shoulders showed plainly the marks of the collar and on the feet of each remained a pair of old shoes to help them – once more over the hills they had so often travelled – on the way to market.

How often Rarey must have come upon pathetic cases of doomed or abused horses, while searching among the stables. Some people when faced with overwhelming scenes of suffering, shut down their feelings and become indifferent. Rarey chose to push on and do what he could through his lectures to arouse more respect for horses. From his earliest days he had felt 'an intense fondness' for horses, looking upon them as friends.

Travelling north from Sweden, Rarey met in Lapland an ancient partner of mankind, and Santa Claus – the reindeer. He handled a few of them, and was fascinated by their gentleness, and the comparison in size to the taller elks in America. After this, he continued onward to the Frozen Sea, covering the icy expanses by foot, boats and sledge, reaching a point about fifty miles beyond the Arctic Circle.

By the middle of November, the compass was pointing south, for their ship was moving through the waters back to the coasts of the British Isles. *Sporting Magazine* commented that Rarey had 'returned from his visit to the regions of thick, ribbed ice, looking remarkably strong and well'. Rarey was glad to be back, and when he visited the stables on Kinnerton Street, no doubt he was filled with happiness to see Cruiser's fuzzy horse face looking out from his box. Animals have a wonderful way of releasing a great burst of joy within us when we first see them after being away.

In December, *Sporting Magazine* mentioned that Rarey was regularly riding Cruiser now and 'we are informed that it is the highest ambition of Argus to ride Cruiser. We trust he may ere long present himself to his friend Cruising down Rotten Row [from *route du roi* or King's Road – a riding path in Hyde Park] as no one deserves a ride better, as he first, at the risk of having manslaughter on his conscience for life, dared Mr Rarey to the deed.' It would

Cruising down Rotten Row (*Rarey's Art of Taming Horses*)

have been interesting to see Argus and Rarey meet face to face. As to cruising down Rotten Row, unfortunately no further word was given as to whether it ever happened.

In the closing days of January, 1859, the news came that on the 27th, Victoria, the Princess Royal – now Princess Frederick William of Prussia, had delivered a son. The labour was extremely difficult, a breech birth, and grave fears were raised that both mother and child would be lost. The baby's arm was dislocated in the delivery, but he was otherwise healthy. He was given the name Wilhelm. Later he became known during World War I as Kaiser Wilhelm II.

In early February, Rarey was preparing to travel abroad again, this time to Germany. Ottensin, in Hamburg, was the homeland of his grandfather Carl Rorig. In 1767, Rorig had sailed to America when he was twenty-three-years old. He worked as a dry goods merchant, then tried tenant farming in Maryland and Virginia. He anglicized his name to Charles Rarey and in 1778 married Margaret Wolfe, whose parents had emigrated from England. They moved to Ohio in 1806 as one of the pioneer families in the area; and had eleven children, one dying in infancy. Charles Rarey's restless push to create his own destiny by launching his career in another country came full circle as his grandson John S. Rarey stepped onto the soil of Germany.

In Berlin, Rarey was scheduled to give a private exhibition for the Royal Family of Germany at the King's Riding School. On Tuesday 15 February, the Prince Regent, Prince Frederick William, the Duke of Saxe-Coburg and Gotha, and other members of nobility came to the demonstration.

Sporting Magazine reported that one of the horses brought out was a

> thoroughly spoiled, large, powerful race-horse. He was considered very savage; would bite at anyone who came near him, and was governed with the greatest difficulty by his groom. He was rabid when first introduced into the enclosure, but about a half hour of taming made a great change in him, so much so, that he allowed Mr Rarey to handle him as he pleased; he played with his hind and fore legs, led him first with a straw and then made him follow without leading.
>
> The Prince Regent congratulated him most heartily and so did Prince Frederick William, who said this was the second time he had seen him operate, the first being two days before his marriage, when one of the large cream-coloured stallions at the Royal Mews was the subject.

Prince Frederick William also later remarked how he had admired Princess Victoria's serious interest in Rarey's lecture, on that emotional day, just a little over a year before.

Prior to the first public lesson on 16 February, Rarey was introduced to Baron Alexander von Humboldt, the eighty-nine-year-old 'King of Science'. Humboldt was one of the most respected men in the world, pioneering the study of geology and numerous other 'ologies'. Charles Darwin, who would publish his revolutionary book, *The Origin of the Species* this year, in November 1859, credited Humboldt as the inspiration for his career. He referred to him as 'the greatest scientific traveler who ever lived'.

Humboldt and his pet chameleon received a constant flow of visitors from all over the world, at his apartment in a plain two-storey house in Berlin. He seemed now almost as old as the mountains he studied, yet he was immersed in finishing the fifth volume of his masterwork series *Cosmos*, a history of the physical universe.

Upon meeting Rarey, Humboldt remarked with mischievous wit that he hoped Rarey would 'be polite enough to live to be present' at the dinner being held for him after the performance.

Rarey survived, though he had his hands full with a chestnut mare proficient at biting, kicking, striking and squealing whenever her foreleg was handled. Humboldt attended the dinner, relating that he had spent years travelling the Americas, and had always 'considered himself at least half American'. Rarey later said that Baron von Humboldt had 'impressed him more than any other man'.

The last chapter of the Baron's life came to a peaceful close only a few months later. At half past two in the afternoon, on 6 May, he wrote his final sentence, a quote from Genesis: 'Thus the heavens and the earth were finished, and all the host of them.'

Rarey gave two more lectures in Berlin, and such was the public's interest that he was called 'the lion of the season'. His next destination was the kingdom of ice, tears, and grandeur – Russia and her capital, St Petersburg. Rarey had received an invitation to visit Russia from a colonel in the Czar's cavalry – Baron de Wercinski. The horses captured from the Steppes fought domestication to such a degree that men and horses were being killed at an alarming rate. The cavalry officers were interested to see if Rarey's system would have an effect on them.

In St Petersburg, Rarey was directed to call on Baron Meyendorff, equerry to Czar Alexander II. Greeting Rarey at the front door, Meyendorff explained that it was a Russian holiday and that he was just leaving to see the festivities on the Neva, the river which wound past the capital city. Inviting Rarey to take a seat in his sleigh and come along, they were both soon speeding across the snow drawn by three horses harnessed abreast, known as a troika hitch. The outside horses galloped while the middle or shaft horse kept trotting. The middle horse carried the shaft bow – a piece of wood shaped like a rainbow, which attached to the shafts. A merry jingling accompanied the music of hoofbeats, from the bells hung under the peak of the shaft bow. Troikas were initially used for postal and passenger service, but after the railways came, they were mostly reserved for pleasure and holiday rides.

Arriving at the river's edge, Rarey was astonished to see thousands of people gathered to watch the troika races on the ice of the Neva. The oval track for racing was marked on the ice with green fir and cedar branches. The racehorses were a beautiful sight as they came

Troika ice racing on the Neva River in St Petersburg (after a drawing by J. Charlemagne, c. 1850)

prancing, the streamers and tassels on their harness creating dancing splashes of colour.

The crowds came alive with a wild enthusiasm at the start of the races. The exuberant scene was exciting to behold. The novelist Theophile Gautier experienced it, writing in his book, *Voyage in Russia*, published in 1866:

'It is marvellous to watch these magnificent animals, often worth a fortune, speed across the ice…Breath spurts in jets from their scarlet nostrils like smoke; their flanks are bathed in steam and their tails look as if they had been powdered with diamonds.'

The nobility sent their best horses, but anyone could enter. At the races ran when Rarey was in the crowd, an everyday man with three fiery half trained horses fresh from the Steppes won the main event. The jubilant man was carried on a sea of shoulders and presented to the Czar.

After the races, Laplanders with reindeers pulling sleighs came onto the ice to give rides around the track for a few kopecks. 'Loads of jolly pedestrians crowded in', wrote T. B. Thorpe in the *Harper's Magazine* article on Rarey, 'and a group of sleds would move away almost dim with speed. The reindeer were perfectly trained and seemed to enter into the sport with all the spirit of their masters'.

Rarey, intrigued by the Laplanders, visited their camp of tents pitched on the ice. He saw reindeer and sheep lying contentedly by the outside flaps of the tents, while inside, children played and slept amidst the furs spread on the icy ground.

Rarey's next adventure in Russia began a few days later with a command from the Czar. He was invited to try his system on a dangerous horse roaming free in a deer-park at an imperial preserve. No one could do anything with this horse, a gift from the Cossacks, so he had been turned loose there. Rarey went to the preserve with Colonel Lefter, head of the government horse department, and two officers. He asked for the horse to be herded into an enclosure, which proved a difficult task. Finally the horse was in, a barricade was built in front of the door, and then Rarey went in alone. During the next two hours, the horse used every man-hating device in his bag of tricks – striking, biting and screaming with a ferocious blast. When at last the door opened, Rarey stood beside the horse, holding the reins. While everyone watched, he saddled the horse, and then trotted off down the road to St Petersburg.

Czar Alexander, amused by the results, ordered a private presentation for the imperial family and members of the court. In the *Harper's* article, Thorpe wrote about the uproar when the signal was given to begin, and a 'perfectly wild brute from the Steppes' came charging into the riding arena.

Attempting to anchor the horse were two men

themselves semi-barbarous, awed by the presence of the Emperor and filled with intense fear by the plunging and rearing of the horse in their charge, with difficulty restrained him from breaking away, biting their flesh, or knocking their brains out with his heels, which at times cleaved the air with fearful velocity, for the infuriated animal in the insanity of his captivity, absolutely bit at interposing objects as if he were a tiger.

Mr Rarey, perfectly self-possessed and to the surprise of all present, boldly laid a hand upon his neck, and then passed it gently over the ears, and in a few moments ordered the men to unloose their vigorous hold on the ropes, when Mr Rarey proceeded to further pacify the creature.

The Emperor and the imperial family looked on with amazement, which was quite equal to the mixture of awe and wonder of the two men, and the effect was heightened when the Emperor, half sternly and half playfully asked them, 'Why could they not thus handle the horse?'

The men answered that Rarey must be in cahoots with a force of black magic. Thorpe related that the Emperor and Empress thoroughly enjoyed the presentation, '…entering into the humors of the evening with a hearty abandonment…' What lay ahead for Rarey to explore now was another kingdom, and an entanglement with a king of very odd proportions.

8

THE TRUMPET OF THE KING

CRUISER was sleek and shiny as the spring of 1859 came into full bloom, and John Rarey was hanging his top hat in London again – at 35 Pall Mall. In a respectable section of gentlemen's clubs, Pall Mall was named after the king's game of pell mell, which was similar to croquet.

Number 35, the Adair House, was on the north side of the street. There were 'three lofty storeys', containing several residences owned by lawyers, and a section used as a lodging house for professional men. From here, Rarey could look across the street to see the British Legion and the Army and Navy Club, and just down the way was St James's Square.

At Leicester Square, Rarey booked the Royal Alhambra Palace for a series of lectures. So, he was again searching for rebellious horses to provide the excitement, something he did not particularly care for. Henry Hall Dixon noted that 'if one thing above another has bothered him, it has been the necessity of providing his own subjects…it was not taming savages, but finding them that seemed his greatest difficulty'.

Cruiser was yesterday's news but he would soon prove there was nothing old or stale about him.

In July, Rarey found a new challenge in the form of a dark bay 16.1-hand lop-eared stallion named the King of Oude. In former days, the King could run, even though he had a club foot. He won the Queen's Plate three times during his racing career. He was remembered vividly by some, arriving in the paddock 'in the great hoods he wore to support his ears'.

Pall Mall (*Illustrated London News* 1852)

After he retired to stud, however, he became a monster to handle, once knocking down a groom and ripping the shirt from his back. Nobody would even attempt to put a lead on him until he was 'reduced into submission by thirst'.

Rarey paid £30 for him, and brought him to the stable on Kinnerton Street, where he promptly pulled up a post at the front. Rarey put him on double corn rations to fill out his 'dusty, gaunt frame', and soon he was dancing on tiptoes.

On the night of the King's debut at the Alhambra, the air was crackling with anticipation. *Sporting Magazine* published an article about the evening that was anonymous, but it was probably from the pen of Henry Hall Dixon.

> The King was a rare trumpeter as he stood in his stall near the wings, and it was these loud defiances which worked up the audience so well before he led him in…'Bravo Horse! Bravo Rarey!' counter-shouts rang through the house – it was a glorious scene when the pole was unlocked and Mr Rarey, without a stick or anything but a long leading rein, was left alone with that biting savage in the ring. He fairly swung him round it, as if he was a pony, with an air which seemed to say – 'Come along! Your kingdom has departed from you!'
>
> Ladies too, who are often firmer than men at such times, did not scruple to confess that they trembled all over. He was as nasty with his legs as with his mouth, and the most cat-like activity on Mr Rarey's part was requisite to elude him, as he whisked around.
>
> Mr Rarey tells us he did not find him so bad as Stafford, as he got sooner to his shoulder. That was his great point – he got to his shoulder and he never left it. The horse seemed quite puzzled at his inability to get rid of him, and once, as he bit round in a sort of fury, he fairly seemed to quail at finding the quiet spectre still on guard, and giving him a fixed look, which he dare not face again. We never till that moment thought there was so much influence in a firm man's glance, as there evidently is. The rest was routine after the first 20 minutes… yet – the horse had…fought like a tiger, or as it was once misprinted, 'like a cigar'.

Rarey's next 'cigar' was a horse called Cretingham Hero, stabled in Ipswich. The horse had a reputation as a 'lion rampant', so the Great Eastern Company railway would only ship the horse via a special train with Rarey aboard. As it turned out, the performance with this horse was not a great success. Rarey was quite worn out from the long train ride the day before, and in the arena he had some serious close calls. He narrowly escaped being kicked, and when he went to put his hand in the horse's mouth, it 'roared like a lion'. When he asked the horse to get up, he sat up on his haunches like a dog.

After these embarrassing moments, more was in store. Rarey had announced before the show that he would bring out the King of Oude again, but after he was finished with Cretingham Hero, his arm ached so badly from a severe cramp that he knew it would be useless to try and handle him. And so the audience went home, luke warm.

This was becoming a persistent, dangerous pattern for Rarey, that he would drive himself onward until utterly exhausted. The physical exertion of the demonstrations was enormous, plus all the mental strain of scheduling the performances, finding the horses and then having to work them in front of the critical eye of the public. Like any performer, he was a target for hecklers and jokers who thought it was funny to call out or drop things to scare the horse.

The mental overload certainly was not eased by what happened in the next few days with Cruiser. The papers and tongue-waggers eagerly spread the news that in a flash of his former fury, Cruiser had turned on his groom. The story was exaggerated but the reports were in part true.

Sporting Magazine reported:
Cruiser's faux pas has been a great source of rejoicing to others, but there is a perfect explanation to it. It happened soon after Cretingham Hero arrived; and the three horses [including the King of Oude] were in boxes, placed in one stable of no great size. Cruiser's groom wanted to show off before his country cousin, and he must needs take his horse out of his box, and play tricks in the adjoining riding-school. He was finally laying him down, an operation which the horse does not love, and the smell and challenges of the other stallions working him up, he turned and bit the man's arm once. The trampling on him is all pure fudge; and at first the man did not think that the injury extended beyond a shirt-tear, although it has proved much more severe, and has required very careful treatment. There was no 'heavy wooden gag' near the horse, and the horse seldom wears his wooden bit except when he is cleaned, or is likely to be excited. Mr Rarey has often been absent from him for months together, and yet he has never committed himself before: and it would be strange indeed, and very inconsistent

with the principles of the system, if it had crushed every common feeling out of a horse, so that even teasing and the presence of other stallions would not rouse him. However, we will warrant that Mr Rarey cares as little for being 'savaged' on paper, as he does for meeting any savage face to face in the ring that either friend or foe can find.

Rarey found himself at the cavalry barracks next, after his series at the Alhambra ended, teaching the riders, trainers, grooms and farriers there. For the rest of the summer and into the autumn, Rarey and Cruiser were travelling about the British Isles on a lecture tour. On 24 September, they were in the sea side resort of Brighton, the 'horse-ridingest city in creation'.

Working their way north, by mid-October they crossed the border into Scotland. They continued on to the fascinating capital city of Edinburgh, located on the Firth of Forth.

Rarey wrote down his thoughts while there, in a small red leather journal. The main focus of Rarey's mind wherever he went was horses, and such he wrote about in the little beige pages.

Rarey's journal with his writings about the Edinburgh kicking mare in 1859 (Photo by author. Courtesy Anne and Ed Rarey, Groveport, Ohio)

Under the headline 'Chestnut Kicking Mare Thursday October 17 Edinburgh' he began:

> This afternoon about 2 o'clock I took the above mare in hand at Scots Riding School. The bake harness and a steady horse were prepared for me. I first put up the right fore foot and gave her a little exercise, with only a snaffle bridle, without blinds or winkers.
>
> At first she did not know what to do. As soon as I began to move her, she could not stand the light, moving, tickling sensation of the hip straps. I could not blame her for that, she only wanted those tickling, unpleasant straps away from her. I kept stroking her a good deal with my hand, then asked her to move on. She promenaded on three legs with a wicked kick between every hop. She kept kicking so I let her, it was doing no harm…It was a slight difference in our wants and opinions as to which it should be that was all.
>
> So I paid not attention to the kicking, without a blow or jerk at the bit, or even without a sour look, for she labored under a disadvantage to kick with both hind feet and only one fore leg to stand on. I didn't do this to exhaust her strength for then she would probably throw herself down and have turned stubborn and thus defeated all my plans.
>
> I had an object in view in doing all this, which was to work all the freshness out of her or to use an expressive term, 'to work off the edge' and make her a little more steady and not quite so frisky.
>
> I must here say to my friends of the prevention of cruelty to animals, which is a principle which guides all my actions, that this perspiration of the mare was only caused by exercise the same as horse trainers sweat their horses by giving them running exercise until the water drops off them – which makes the flesh hard and enables them to run a race without showing fatigue. I believe this is no more punishment than the man who labors until perspiration stands upon his face, which does both man and horse good. So far from being a cruelty, is good and conducive to good health, good feeling and good appetite.

After a while, the mare gave up her kicking and went quietly. Humility is a boat on the river of knowledge, and Rarey certainly took a few rides in that boat. For in the midst of writing about this chestnut kicking mare he mentioned: 'I can now see the many mistakes I have made learning the secret of horse taming.'

THE EYE OF THE HURRICANE

LASGOW was their next city stop. *The Glasgow Gazette* on 22 October 1859 published its impressions of Rarey and Cruiser:

> In appearance Mr Rarey is decidedly prepossessing being about 5 feet 9 inches in height, light haired, light complexioned, with intelligent eyes, an open countenance and a manner that won the audience from the moment that he raised his hat and unaffectedly acknowledged their plaudits. He is singularly young for the noise he has made in the world, his age being only 31…As for Cruiser, he is a fine thoroughbred animal, conscious of the admiration he is accustomed to excite, but without any indication of vice about him.

Cruiser seemed to be enjoying life on the road. What a bright change from his former days of staring at the same walls – day after day. It was the thoughts of all the other Cruisers still out there, rotting away in dark stalls; sullen, dejected and dangerous, which kept Rarey on the road, talking and talking about horses. Sometimes, he even gave demonstations without charge. Before he left Glasgow, he gave a free lecture to the cabmen of the city.

In early November, Rarey was back in England, and appeared on the 9th at the Alhambra. This performance proved to be one of his most difficult trials yet, thanks to a powerful thoroughbred who was as nasty as he was big. This stallion was determined to fight every effort to handle him, by kicking, biting and rearing straight up and slashing through the air with his hooves.

A journalist for the *Illustrated London News* wrote that the horse:

tore to pieces every strap put upon him, hurling to the ground the groom who had come to Mr Rarey's assistance. At one time the horse broke completely away and stood for a moment a victor in the midst of the excited audience. Two men came to Mr Rarey's aid, but they were unable to hold the animal which scattered men and everything else around him like chaff...

Mr Rarey approached the horse and as there were no signs of trembling in Rarey, we trembled for him. Then began a contest which no one who witnessed it can ever forget. It was a struggle of art and tact against overwhelming strength. Now the man had gained the mastery, now the horse. The animal touching the earth seemed to derive fresh strength. At last Rarey extemporized a strap from the fragments of a broken bridle and gained his first steps to progress. Still the horse fought fiercely, rising and plunging in all directions, endeavouring to bite his tamer or trample him down...

The contest blazed for an hour and a half, then at last, the horse stood calmly while Rarey finished his lecture from the horse's back. *Sporting Magazine* later mentioned that: 'Rarey confessed afterwards that he thought it was hopeless, but his face was no index to that feeling. Be the difficulty what it might, there was a calmness about him which always reassured you.'

The *Illustrated News of the World* had commented in the summer of 1859 that Rarey was the eye in the middle of the hurricane on stage. When a savage Suffolk cart horse that had once killed a groom was brought in, the lower rows of the audience began to clear out in case the chestnut giant should

take a fancy to leap among the spectators. But there was Rarey, standing coolly within a yard of the bad character's heels. He merely observed that the most dangerous part of this horse's disposition was that it kicked and bit without giving any warning by laying its ears back...

Any man who has the same cool, fearless nature as Mr Rarey may do as he does, but where are you to find that man? Who could advance fearlessly to the mouth of the murderous biter, or stand calmly by the side of the heaving, raging kicker?

Before the hobbles and the straps are required the nerves must be educated. No sense of danger must disturb the operator. His temper must never be roused but the soft, patting hand and kind voice must be ready to soothe...Before he proceeds to strap up the leg of a horse, he always passes his hand gently over the creature's body, and so by degrees reaches the leg he wishes to hold...Mr Rarey always tells his pupils that when they stroke a horse, they should pass the hand over him as lightly as if caressing a bird.

The winter birds were now huddling for warmth as the December holidays drew closer. On 21 December, Rarey received a note from the artist John Leech saying, 'Sir Edwin Landseer will be happy to see you after next Monday (26 December) any afternoon after 4 o'clock.'

It is not known whether John Leech initiated the idea for them to meet, or if Landseer was curious about the young horseman. Whatever the reason, it must have been exciting for Rarey to shake the hand of Sir Edwin Landseer.

Wrapped inside ordinary features, he was a genius with colour and a brush. An extraordinary animal artist, the horses, dogs, and stags on his canvases glowed with a powerful living radiance. His long career included the lion sculptures at the base of the Nelson Monument in Trafalgar Square, and many portraits of the Royal Family. He had given sketching lessons to Queen Victoria who felt his artwork was 'perfect'.

As the 1850s gave way to the new decade, Rarey was in the news again on 9 January, for meeting, training, and gentling a relative of Cruiser. This dark bay stallion was named Pine Apple, and true to the family temper, had also been sentenced to wear an iron muzzle.

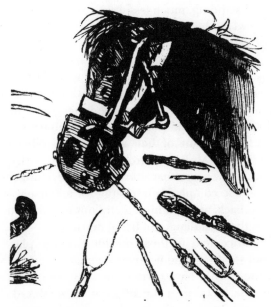

In mid-January, Rarey held a free lecture for cabmen and omni-bus drivers at Allen's Riding School, owned by Mr Fred Allen, a respected riding master. The atmosphere surrounding the lecture was captured vividly by *Sporting Magazine*, again most likely by Henry Hall Dixon, published in March 1860.

By half past eight, Seymour Street seemed blocked up by strings of cabs; but a fare might have hailed them in vain. The steeds stood ruminating in the shafts; some few happier ones deep in their nose bags, while the drivers had hurried down the line, and cast in their fortunes among the surging sea of heads, which struggled towards the door of the Riding School, tightly grasping their badge, as the Open Sesame of the evening.

There was a novelty about the invitation, which seemed to have tickled them, and at least three to four hundred never got into the building at all. The audience consisted of about 2500, among whom three quarters were cabmen or omni-bus drivers, while the remainder were made up of friends with 'a stable mind', who had borrowed the badge for the evening, and stood treat for the privilege.

The reporters of the different papers had seats allotted them in the centre, and a few private friends of Mr Rarey's—Mr Lemon and Mr Leech—surveyed the scene from the window of Mr Allen's office, which opens into the Riding School, and quite served from its elevation, all the purposes of a grandstand.

Within five minutes after the doors were opened, it was hopeless either to find standing, much less sitting, room; and as nothing could keep the crowd on the floor from encroaching too much on the arena, the line of sight suffered still more. We heard one cabman most pathetically lamenting his inability to see more than the horse's crest at intervals, over his fellows, and vow that he would sooner have paid five shillings and seen everything, than walk his five miles and see nothing…a few set ladders against the inner wall and climbed onto them, others…with the aid of a friendly shoulder sat bodily on the neck of any 'gentle giant' of their acquaintance. When every resource failed, they lionized Mr Rarey's groom, and heard, with quiet attention, the fact from his own lips, that after one day's teaching, he was enabled to take the horse completely in charge for a journey of 800 miles to Glasgow and back, and put him in and out of railway trains unaided, and without the least danger of being devoured.

The announcement to those outside that the place was full was anything but soothing, and it almost seemed as if with a series of wolf-like yells, they would have carried the very doors by assault…Select knots, it is true, stood near the adjacent 'Palaces' and chaffed divers passers-by with 'Here comes Mr Rarey!' while the street boys joined in the horse laugh at their senior's wit, and sang how 'Mr Rarey, got down the airee'; but the mind of the British cabmen felt permanently relieved with their rallies, and the ever faithful half and half did the rest...

A more quiet and attentive audience, on the whole, no man could have desired. When Cruiser came in and when he went out, they cheered lustily; and, in fact, it was from these little outbursts of feeling alone, that the outsiders gathered that the horse was either down or showing good fight.

The chestnut of Mr Allen's was a very pretty subject, and did not give in without a very dashing contest. The cart horse, although not exactly coming up to Mr Rarey's definition of 'a proud and lively savage', after sundry kickings and squealings, had all its disinclination to allow any one to get on its back, effectually overcome in half an hour.

On the whole, the evening was a most satisfactory one, the audience showed their appreciation of it by 'a cheer for Rarey', as they left. Unlike so many of the groom world, they have never looked on that gentleman as a standing reproof to them and their ways, and hence they just came to see what there was to be seen, without any scepticism or previous grudge.

In fact, from the purely elementary questions we heard many of them put to each other, we should fancy that they had hardly given the system or its operator a thought before. They have merely looked on Mr Rarey as a horse tamer, and nothing else; and then as 'they're pretty well tamed afore they come to us', they didn't take much heed to him. Mr Rarey, however, thought differently, and dealt especially with the folly of overflogging horses; and as, of course, everyone scorned to take the hint as meant for himself, they acquiesced with him en masse. He left town on the next Tuesday, and gave two exhibitions in Paris on his way to the East– to watch the Eastern mode of horse handling.

In Paris, one of his lectures was attended by the writer Theophile Gautier, who in the *Le Moniteur Universal* on 21 January 1860, brought up some important considerations:

Are the animals subdued for long or permanently? The lesson forgotten, will they return to their former character? Will another than Rarey be able to effectively apply the system? I am unable to say, and experience only can answer the questions. What pleases me in the method of this American is that it is humane – no nose torture, no bridling, no whip with cutting thongs, no spurs with sharp points, no post of suffering, nothing but kindness – the moral victory...

Cab and horse (*Illustrated London News*)

Whether Rarey's system produced a lasting change or a temporary one was a valid question. Cruiser's transformation seemed to prove an emphatic yes, but he was with Rarey the majority of the time. Cruiser was cooperative, but not overly submissive. His stallion self-esteem and readiness to defend himself were securely intact, as his one groom painfully found out.

What about other horses? A race-mare Rarey handled in 1858 named Miss Finch, had been a first class two-year-old until her temper became so fierce she was dangerous to start. After Rarey's lessons, she was able to be ridden again, but she never equalled her previous speed. Whether this was due to Rarey's process or a hundred other possibilities such as unsoundness or lack of fitness cannot be determined. The merit in making a violent horse safer to handle, and even saving the lives of horses about to be destroyed for aggression, would seem to outweigh the demerits of diminished speed. But why should Rarey's method slow a horse's speed? Horses lie down and roll every day. It is possible though, that the horse's knees could be damaged if it went down on them with too much force.

How do the results with horses compare with those with the zebra? Fred Taylor, the loyal supporter of Rarey's early rival, James Telfer, wanted to test whether Rarey's system was lasting. He paid a visit to the zebra Rarey had worked with, who was back at the zoo. Unfortunately, the zebra was being kept in a small enclosure tended by an unmerciful keeper, who continually poked the zebra with a pointed pole. When Taylor came near though, the zebra pushed his nose through the slats to be petted, and seemed to enjoy the contact. Taylor concluded that Rarey's system had brought a lasting change in this poor black and white fellow.

Rarey's thoughts were turning now to the East. He had been curious about the Arabs and their mysterious bond with their horses ever since he had read books about them as a child. He wondered whether the reality would match the stories and what he would find in those ancient cities and the shifting sands of the Sahara.

10

EXPLORING THE MYSTERIES OF THE MIDDLE EAST

*B*IDDING au revoir to Paris, Rarey and a small group of friends set off to the lands of ancient mysteries. On the first leg of the trip, they visited Rome. There, Rarey noted in his journal that most Italian horses wore shoes only on their front feet. This was the same as Cruiser, whose hind feet were in good condition and Rarey 'did not want to ruin them with shoes'. In lectures though, he recommended that young horses working in the streets should have shoes, so they don't get tender feet and become fearful of going forward.

Saying goodbye to Rome with a fond *arrivederci*, they went south to Naples, past Mount Vesuvius. This smoking volcano which had buried Pompeii in AD 79, still angrily shot forth flames and lava from time to time. They stopped next at Sicily and Malta, and then went to Alexandria. Cleopatra's Needles, the two stone structures or obelisks, were still pointing to the sky above Alexandria after some 3000 years. On the other side of the city, stood Pompey's Pillar, an enormous slab of pink granite 27 feet wide and 86 feet long.

By mid February, they were floating down the longest river in the world – the Nile – where Rarey at last was able to see Arabian horses in their native lands. The graceful grey, chestnut and bay horses were quietly munching grass while tethered to stakes.

The ship soon came to Cairo, the capital city of Egypt, a city surrounded by walls and palm-tree gardens. Cairo was once the home of Abbas Pacha, reputedly one of the greatest breeders of Arabian horses since King Solomon. After his death, his 'unequalled stud' of some 300 Arabians was put up for auction in Cairo in 1860, by his eighteen-year-old son, Haleem Pacha.

After a brief stay, Rarey and his friends journeyed to the west bank of the Nile, to Giza, to see the magnificent Sphinx and the Pyramids. The Pyramids could only be reached in those days via a donkey caravan.

Returning to Alexandria, they now travelled east to Jerusalem. There by an olive tree, a military official asked Rarey to inspect four Arabian mares of the 'purest Nedgedee caste'. One mare was so precious to the official, he would not even consider an offer of 1,000 pounds for her.

Moving on again, this time into the vicinity of the Dead Sea, the carefree mood of the travellers was dimmed by an unsettling event. In her book, *Rarey, the Horse's Master and Friend,* Sara Lowe Brown relates that a gang of thieves

> descended on the tent and cooking utensils, made the cook stand and deliver his watch, and maltreated the solitary soldier for saucily remonstrating. Mr Rarey and his party were some miles ahead at the time; but the former learned from the incident the lesson of caution and left all of his possessions in Damascus when later, accompanied only by Major Frazer, of lion hunting fame, and an interpreter, he spent several days in the desert in search of horse lore, riding up to every encampment he could descry and trusting for food and a night's lodging to the sheiks of the villages.

Rarey's experiences here were also chronicled in an American newspaper, *The Boston Traveller,* by an anonymous correspondent [the Boston friend Mr Robson?]. The article was reprinted in the *Ohio State Journal* on 12 June 1860, with a dateline Beirut, 29 March.

> Our distinguished countryman, Mr J. S. Rarey...has been spending some time in the desert of Arabia, among the Arabs and their fine horses...he has toured from Jaffa to Jerusalem, thence to Damascus via Samaria and the Sea of Galilee, then to Beirut by way of Baalbess.
>
> He made several detours into the desert to search for the great tribes of Bedouins who hang among the borders of Syria and Palestine...His pursuits after the Bedouin camps however, were unsuccessful. A three-days ride into the desert convinced him that they were more than a 20 days journey beyond the Jordan, so he abandoned the search, contenting himself with seeing all the Arabian horses in Jerusalem, Damascus, and Beirut.

In Beirut, Mr Rarey received every attention to which his reputation entitled him, and the American and European consuls treated him with a great respect. Invitations to dinners crowded upon him in such numbers that he was forced to decline some of them for want of time.

[In Syria]…the US Consul Mr Johnson, introduced Rarey to Ayoub Bey, who presented William H. Seward of New York, while visiting this country last summer with three fine Arabian horses. Ayoub Bey claimed them to have the best blood in Syria, so our Consul was anxious to obtain Mr Rarey's opinion upon these horses soon to be shipped to Auburn, New York.

Bey ordered out two of the horses, one was absent in the mountains, and they were trotted up and down the paved courtyard to the delight of those gathered. Mr Rarey, after examining them thoroughly, declared himself better pleased with them than any others seen in Syria. One colt is two years, the other a large bay of seven years…were pronounced to be a remarkably fine collection…

The American residents here were gratified at the visit of Mr Rarey not only because he received attention from consuls and Pachas as an American, but from the pleasure afforded them by a personal acquaintance with the man. Modest and unassuming, and at the same time frank and cordial, he pleased everyone, and convinced the Syrian world that an American can be celebrated without blowing his own trumpet, and great without pretensions.

His conversation never 'smells of the shop' for the subject of his great study-the horse – is never mentioned by himself in society; but when the subject is introduced by others, he converses freely, but without conveying the impression that he supposes his opinion more valuable than that of others, or that he is 'the' Mr Rarey who has the crowned heads of Europe for his auditors…Rarey declares that he controls horses by no great secret or any personal influence, but by a system at once simple and natural which can be practised by others as well as by himself…Having left Syria now for Cyprus, Rhodes, and Constantinople, he will no doubt find much to interest him in the latter place while exercising his skill in the stables of the Sultan.

Soon they were sailing into the Sea of Marmara, and arrived in Constantinople, where Rarey proceeded to see the Sultan at the Topkapi Palace. Inside the luxurious rooms, during the pleasantries, Rarey was offered a pipe to smoke which had diamonds set into the amber mouthpiece.

The Turkish Sultan was on the throne of the Ottoman Empire and the capital was Constantinople, a city straddling two continents – Europe and Asia. People had been living in this ancient city with its steep cobblestone lanes, since about 3,000 BC. Horses had always been a valued centrepiece of the culture. Passionate chariot races had once been held there at the Greek hippodrome, the largest one ever built.

Rarey visited several of the leading breeding farms there, finding the horses to be handled and trained in an admirable manner. His adventures in the mysterious Middle East and the deserts of Arabia had been exciting and memorable, but the sand was running quickly through the hourglass. It was time to go home – first to England, then to America.

He was planning a farewell tour of the British Isles, during the summer and autumn; then in November, he'd cross the Atlantic once more and introduce Cruiser to the not-so-United States.

Cruiser, during this time, had been passing along his famous bloodlines. For he was advertised in 1860 as standing at stud at Althorpe Paddocks in England. He had a lot of good physical qualities to give future generations, for J. H. Walsh in *The Horse in the Stable and the Field* described the sons of Venison as having 'Arabian looking heads, fine muzzles, full eyes, light necks, good shoulders, wiry and lasting legs and feet, light girth, and a want of weight for the legs to carry'. Mares with 'the Venison crest' were said to be bay with a shot of white hairs.

The year had now revolved to the month of May, a favourite with horses for the soft air, green growing grass, freedom from blankets, and a good roll on the warm ground. In the middle of the month on 16 May, Henry Hall Dixon's birthday, Rarey was honoured with the presentation of a medal from the Royal Association for the Prevention of Cruelty to Animals, the RSPCA, at St James's Hall in Piccadilly. The honest purpose behind his work for horses clearly shone in the words he spoke upon receiving the medal, which were given in Sara Lowe Brown's book *The Horse Cruiser*.

Ladies and Gentlemen – I am not in the habit of appearing before a public audience without a horse by my side. (Cheers and Laughter) I am far more a man of action than of words. I can only say I have long been led to believe that a horse was unnecessarily ill treated in training because we do not understand his nature as it has grown up in his native pasture, and as it can only be understood where horses are reared extensively.

My father reared them and I had a good opportunity of studying them in a way that you cannot study them in boxes or stalls, but where we see them in a state of nature...I have always admired the noble animal, and thought it was a great pity that a horse could not be trained without the violence which is generally employed. I have seen them in the pasture feeding with cattle and sheep – I have seen that they have no fear of other animals, and I have wondered why they should have that fear of man. I thought there must be friendship existing between the horse and man, as between the horse and other animals...

I have lately been in Arabia, where the horse grows up with the man, and I have had no difficulty in taking them by the mane. I have seen the people drinking camel's milk, and they always give a portion to their horse, so that they grow up together in good will, kindness, and good feeling; and if all people managed and understood the horse and felt for him as they do, you would scarcely need any laws of punishment for cruelty to the horse...

    I have had to encounter violent prejudices and oppositions, but I am most thankful to your Lordship [Sir John Scott Lillie] for the complimentary manner in which you have spoken of my own efforts. I am thankful also for the compliment you have paid to my people. I believe when the heart is right, it does not matter whether we are Americans or Englishmen. When we understand one another, like the Arab and his horse, we may all be mutual friends...

By the end of May, during the week of Queen Victoria's birthday, 24 May, Rarey was lecturing again at the Alhambra. His performances were still popular, and tickets went at a rapid rate. John Leech sent a note to him dated 26 May beginning 'May I trespass upon your friendship again...', requesting three seats at Rarey's lecture that day, and extending an invitation to dinner the following evening.

    The days were pleasant but busy, and soon he and Cruiser were riding the rails again. In June, Rarey was talking about horses in Leeds, a town in Yorkshire famous as a 'centre of hog enthusiasm'.

    In J. B. Booth's biography, *Bits of Character: A Life of Henry Hall Dixon, The Druid* he noted that '...the pig is the very axis of the locality. At dinner-time the men devote a half an hour rigidly to the sties. They sit and scratch their grunting idols if it is wet, and they walk them out if it is fine;...and the best blanket in the house is freely given up for the candidate pig.'

    As one porcine sportsman related, 'A bit of good Pig-Racing is worth all your horse running business. It's twice the fun and a hundredth part of the expense.'

John Leech (Sketch by James Souder)

In this piggie-loving town, Rarey felt prompted to respond in writing to a question brought up during his lecture by a Mr Callahan.

Mr Callahan   June 13, 1860

Dear Sir,
    The vicious mare which was subdued at my lecture yesterday, was very intelligent, and much more manageable than a stupid horse. If I had time to give her a few lessons, she would become quite gentle.
                        I am Dear Sir,
                        Yours Truly
                        J. S. Rarey

Reproduced by permission of the Ohio Historical Society,
Columbus, Ohio

Around the end of June, Rarey discovered something that really caught his eye and his heart – the Shetland pony. While visiting the blustery Shetland Islands, some 200 miles above the top of Scotland, where sometimes the wind is so strong that people, cows and boats are blown right into the air, Rarey was instantly fascinated by the clever, tiny ponies. He purchased five of them, and gave one to an Englishman there, who had often extended a hand to American

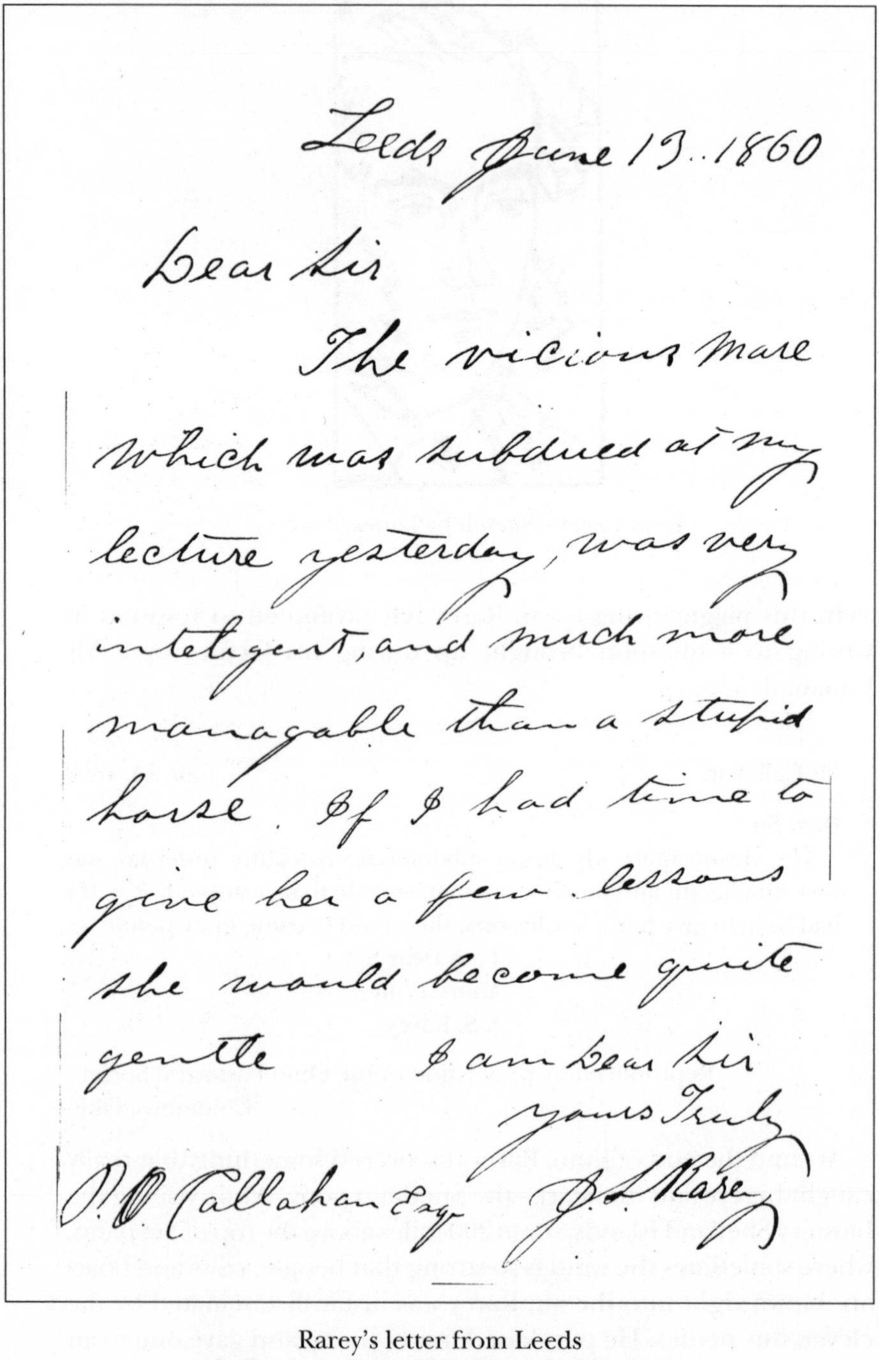

Leeds June 19..1860

Dear Sir

The vicious mare
which was subdued at my
lecture yesterday, was very
inteligent, and much more
managable than a stupid
horse. If I had time to
give her a few. lessons
she would become quite
gentle   I am Dear Sir
           yours Truly
P.P. Callahan Esq   J.S. Rarey

Rarey's letter from Leeds
(Collection of the Ohio Historical Society)

travellers. The rest he brought back with him to London.

By the first week of July he was giving lessons again at the Riding House on Motcombe Street. The lectures were lively as usual, for a letter he received from William Man Jr on 26 July began: 'I am glad to learn you are safe and sound in spite of the risks you have been running...'

One risk he was not taking was marriage. His family said he was 'a favourite with the ladies', and he did receive a lot of attention from women who appreciated his looks, gentlemanly qualities and healthy bank account. He chose though, to remain single. We can only guess at his reasons. One consideration may have been the prospect of a sudden death from his dangerous occupation. He certainly gave this some thought, for he had a will drawn up in England. And as he was constantly travelling with his shows, marriage and a family life would have been difficult to sustain.

On the subject of marriage, it's interesting to wonder whether Rarey received any advice from his friend Henry Hall Dixon. Dixon was happily married to Caroline Lynes, and they had thirteen children. Unfortunately two died shortly after birth and four others succumbed to childhood diseases. Dixon, with so many heads around the table, struggled constantly to earn enough money to ensure their care and comfort. He was writing constantly for newspapers, magazines, and authoring books; but a literary career is not often a lucrative one. And he was a generous man. He had taken the time to help further Rarey's career, even with all his responsibilities pressing upon him. First he gave him favourable publicity with frequent updates in his columns, and later he assisted him with business account work.

Rarey tried to give Dixon some money to repay him for his time and effort, but Dixon would not hear of it. Mrs Dixon later recalled in an interview with *Livestock Journal* in 1927:

> Henry's indifference to money has not been exaggerated in the least. I often wish it had been...Rarey was quite an uneducated man, and he could never have gained all the reputation he did without my husband's assistance. Henry managed everything for him, and would never take a penny for all the work he did, hard as Rarey pressed him. When he could not move Henry, Rarey came to me, and I shall never forget the curious way he tried to give me the money he quite rightly declared he owed us.
>
> Our drawing room in Kensington Square was a large double room

Henry Hall Dixon (*Orkneys to Kensington* by Dixon)

with curtains and a step in between; if you were sitting in one room there might be somebody in the other without you knowing it. Rarey came one afternoon while I was at the writing table; he looked stealthily around and then took a little bag of gold from his pocket and threw it to me along the polished floor. Henry, who unknown to us both, was in the other room, heard it, and was up at once. 'Give that back,' he said before I had time to touch it. Rarey looked very crestfallen; so did I, no doubt.

Foiled again, Rarey went back to his apartment to think of a new plan. He really enjoyed his home away from home there, for as Henry Hall Dixon later wrote: 'Many a merry party there was of all nations at 35 Pall Mall...One of his leading dinner ideas was producing cans of preserved peaches from "the old house at home" whose photograph he cherished in all his wanderings.'

And soon he would be back walking among those peach orchards again, but it would not be the same. For America was rumbling with a violent discontent, which was shaking the country all the way to her very foundations – the union of her states. The question put forth in the autumn of 1860 was not if she would erupt, but when.

11

A FULL CIRCLE
FAREWELL

*A*S THE American presidential elections drew near, the clash of wills between North and South over economics, slavery, and states rights was raging. Rarey must have been worried about everyone at home, as he was travelling about tying up loose ends, giving lectures such as that at Worcester on 20 September.

In Ohio, feelings ran passionately against slavery, and the majority were loyal to the Union. Rarey's family supported the Republican party, whose candidate for president was the man with the size 14 shoes, the 'almost gigantic' 6 foot 4 inch Abraham Lincoln. Lincoln had ignited the hatred of the South with his public stand against slavery. He recognized their position, but as he said, 'When I hear anyone arguing for slavery, I feel a strong impulse to see it tried on him personally.'

Into this storm of events came an English shaft of sunshine, the eighteen-year-old Prince of Wales, Edward Albert, who had arrived for a tour of North America. After visiting Canada, the royal entourage stopped to see Niagara Falls. They witnessed there an incredible performance by Blondin (Jean-François Gravelet), the fearless French tightrope walker. As Blondin was about to cross over the roaring waters of the Falls on a tightrope, the Prince of Wales remarked, 'For heaven's sake, don't do anything extraordinary because I am here.'

Blondin replied, 'Your Royal Highness, I'll carry you across if you wish.'

The Prince of Wales thanked him, but declined the offer. When

Blondin reached the other side, the Prince with a sigh of relief exclaimed, 'Thank God it is all over.' Later the same afternoon, Blondin crossed again on stilts.

Travelling on, the Prince visited several American cities in October, enduring the 'burning heat and penetrating dust of railway travel with unflagging spirits'. He spent three days in Washington DC as the guest of President James Buchanan, and then went on to New York City. Enthusiastic crowds greeted him, as people thronged to see a man of royalty. A grand torch light parade was held with 'bright, dancing masses of torches, the waving of handkerchiefs, the clapping of hands, and the scene grew more brilliant and exciting every minute', said the *New York Times*.

The Prince stayed at the 5th Avenue Hotel, and in the evening, people gathered below his balcony, waiting for him to appear. While in the city, he visited Brady's Studio to have photographs taken, and stopped by P. T. Barnum's American Museum on Broadway. Barnum's collection was, the London papers reported, 'filled with all sorts of vulgar monstrosities and curiosities'. A few days later, the Prince of Wales sailed for England and thereafter resumed his studies at Oxford.

Rarey meanwhile, was teaching a series of classes for the British

Cavalry horse and man

cavalry at Aldershot. There was a sense of things coming full circle, for he had come to England on the strength of recommendations from the cavalry officers that his system would be 'valuable for military purposes'. And it was.

The *Illustrated London News* reported on 20 October that

The success of his first 25 pupils has been very marked, and the system has been carried out so patiently and effectively by them, that in the regiments from which they were selected, horses of the most refractory kind have been generally put into the ranks at the end of three days. Mr Rarey has been giving a lecture at Crawley, for the funds of the rifle corps, and his last public exhibition in the neighborhood of London will take place at the Crystal Palace on Saturday the 27th, when Cruiser takes his farewell before he crosses the Atlantic in company with four Shetland ponies. One of the latter is so small that Mr Rarey intends to train it to run after him and lie in his room like a Newfoundland dog.

On 27 October some 8,000 people crowded into the Crystal Palace at Sydenham Hill. Illuminated by gas lights, the nineteen-acre glass building glowed like a huge firefly. Inside, the zero hour that Rarey had been dreading, his last performance in England, had come.

When he walked onto the stage that evening, how difficult it was to hold back emotions on hearing the heartfelt roar of ovation; especially when Cruiser came playfully trotting into the lights, and the cheers began anew.

As in all of Rarey's shows, everyone was anxious to see him handling a rebellious horse, and the more it rebelled, the better. And for this special night, he found a lively one.

An article in *Frank Leslie's Illustrated Newspaper* (New York) on 8 December said:

> The most furious subject at Mr Rarey's last exhibition was an Irish mare, whose screams filled the transept before she was brought in. She was a powerful gray roan; and kicked, bit, reared and howled in the most ferocious manner. Watching his opportunity, Mr Rarey got his strap on her fetlock and finally overthrew her, to the delight of the vast audience, who at one time feared that she might get the better of his cool courage and patience in her efforts to eat him up.

A footnote to his Crystal Palace performance appeared in the *Illustrated London News* on 10 November: 'His encounter with the mare, Maid of Erin, formed a worthy finale to his British campaign against the proud and lively savages…and he sails with Cruiser for America in the course of a fortnight.'

Besides Cruiser and the ponies, Rarey was bringing along 'Thetis, a blood mare' he had purchased from Rawcliffe Farm; thorough-breds were generally known as blood horses.

Something he had commissioned to remember his years here, was also coming home with him – a three-quarter length portrait of himself standing by his right-hand 'man' Cruiser. The artist was Miner Kellogg, an American painter working in Florence, Paris, London, and the East as a diplomatic courier for the United States government. Kellogg later moved back to America, settling after a time in Toledo, Ohio.

There were some other Americans packing to go home this month too; the performers with Howes & Cushing's Great American Circus. Cushing had sold his half of the business to Seth B. Howes in January 1860, but the circus continued, managed by Howes.

After the close of the autumn season, Howes put the circus stock and horses up for auction at Allen's Riding School. On the block were the faithful favourites: Pete and Barney the educated comic mules, the trick horse Black Eagle, and a 'rubber mule', as the clowns call the elephants, named Jenny Lind. Reportedly, one of the bidders at the auction was Joseph Cushing, who purchased the majority of the animals for a new show he was putting together. This circus toured the British Isles for two more years.

As the cold weather crept in during the first week of November, Rarey was finishing his work with the cavalry at Aldershot. The *Illustrated London News* on 1 December, commented on it, saying:

> His Government classes consisted of 50 – half officers and the other half farriers and rough riders. Four or five of them were instructed each day while the rest looked on, kickers and buck jumpers were their principle patients. The previous military system of throwing the horses was for five or six men to tie their legs together, and then fling them violently on one side, but the Rarey–Burghersh strap [Lord Burghersh invented an improved version of Rarey's second strap] has quite done away with this; and saved not a few animals from being turned out of the ranks as hopeless.

Over in the United States, there was a swelling wave of hopelessness on the eve of the election. People were swept up in the emotional storms of secession talk. In the West, all were watching and waiting in anxious limbo to see what would happen. A correspondent for the *New York Times* living in Utah, who said he'd been 'toiling on a slow-motioned mule' sent a dispatch published 8 December saying:

Lincoln elected – Pony Express symbol

The Pony Express folks here have made arrangements to put through the results of the Presidential election in double quick time. So we shall expect to hear, whether the Union is dissolved or compact. Because if it has gone to pieces, what are we to do up in these mountains, so far off, and no good old Uncle Sam to care for us, or give us a 5 cent stick of candy now and then.

To this land of bubbling ferment, Rarey, Cruiser and company were preparing to sail. The ponies breathed the salt of the sea first, leaving in early November. Cruiser and Thetis were scheduled to sail on Friday 23 November, and then Rarey was set to leave the following day from Liverpool.

For horses and ponies, crossing the Atlantic was no pleasure cruise. On one of the upper decks, they were packed like sardines into cramped stalls, designed to deter them from falling during the pitch and roll of the ship. They couldn't brace themselves against the motion, and their hips and shoulders got battered and bruised. There was also the boredom of having nothing new to look at for days on end, the suffocating smell of ammonia, and the misery of sea sickness from the constant movement of the waves.

Waving goodbye is always a wrenching task, and as Rarey's final days in England were dwindling down, he had to tackle this sad business. Henry Hall Dixon later wrote in *Sporting Magazine* that as Rarey was preparing to leave:

> he charged some of his friends, in his simple way, to go and breakfast at his old lodgings, occasionally, just as if he were there, and he seemed quite bothered when they smiled at the idea…

Other friends said goodbye in print. On 1 December, the *Illustrated London News* included an article titled 'The Departure of Mr Rarey', possibly written by his friend Samuel Sidney:

> few can be said to have lived through such an exciting and perilous

three years...he has had the straps on nearly 700 of every shade of temperament. As Emerson says of us, we are a 'nation of centaurs', and hence even a third season found audiences as overflowing and enthusiastic as ever; and the assembly at the Crystal Palace proved that he had not outlived his fame. France furnished a splendid subject in Stafford, and Russia in a Cossack horse, and Cruiser, King of Oude, Pine Apple...were most satisfactory representatives of the savages of the United Kingdom. Strange to say, he carries away no memento except a slight scar on his left hand from the teeth of Stafford...

It is Mr Rarey's intentions to give a few lectures in the States, and then we may see him again in a year's time for one or two exhibitions on his second visit to the different European courts; ready to meet any new incorrigible which arises and neighs its defiance. In the interim, he will principally pass his time on his farm at Groveport, Ohio, collecting material for his book on 'Horse-Taming' and devoting himself to the breeding of bloodstock...

A Champion Highland Society plough is among his purchases, as Indian corn and wheat take up no inconsiderable portion of his tillage ground. The old boarded ring is still there in which from the time he was 12 years old, he began to learn his experience. Cruiser and the Shetland ponies will be taught many a fresh trick in the long summer days.

Few men have been so little spoiled by prosperity, and none ever carried away more completely the general respect and esteem of those with whom he has been connected during his eventful English career.

On Saturday 24 November at 8 am, the Royal Mail Steamship, the Asia, with her crew and Captain Lott at the helm, was weighing anchor at Liverpool and preparing to sail. The ship was carrying the mail, merchandise, and one hundred passengers, one of whom was listed as Mr Rarey.

As the sound of the ship's baritone whistle vibrated in the air, the steamer slowly glided away from the dock. The passengers on deck waved a long frantic farewell to the friends they were leaving behind, people who knew 'the happiness of living in England in the reign of Queen Victoria'.

Twelve days later, nearing the journey's end, his thirty-third birthday came and went quickly away. On the following day, 7 December, in the darkening twilight of a late autumn afternoon, the Asia steamed into the New York harbour and docked at the pier. The hands of the clock in the cabin pointed to 4.30 pm. It was time for the unfolding of a new adventure.

12

NEW YORK, NEW YORK

HE skies were unsettled over New York City on Friday evening. A snow storm was blowing in from the north, while Rarey was checking in to a hotel. On Saturday 8 December, the storm broke. The readers of the *New York Times* opened their papers to read:

> Mr J. S. Rarey, the celebrated horse-tamer, arrived from England in the steamship Asia yesterday afternoon and took rooms at the 5th Avenue Hotel. The notoriety he has gained as a Tamer of wild and vicious horses caused him to be viewed with great curiosity. During the evening, he was the favorite subject of conversation in the parlours of the hotel.

It's strange to think of people whispering about him as he walked briskly by in the lobby, tipping his top hat to the circles of ladies and gentlemen. At the livery stables, Rarey was glad to see that Cruiser, Thetis and the ponies had arrived safely, although Cruiser and the mare had a rather rough passage and their sides were quite tender.

The next step was to find a suitable arena for the lectures. New York had a variety of theatres, but the manager James Nixon convinced Rarey to bring his shows to Niblo's Garden. Niblo's was a popular theatre, attached to the elegant Metropolitan Hotel at the Corner of Broadway and Prince Street. Presently in town at the Bowery Theatre, was the Spaulding and Rogers circus; starring Levi North and 'the Celebrated Dancing Horse' Tammany – the same performers that had been at the Ohio State Fair in Cincinnati in 1850.

Publicity was the key to a big turn-out, and Rarey stirred up interest by offering a reward for vicious horses, promising to select only the worst. Having organized all this business, it was time to go home.

Trains bound for the south or west, travelled from New York to Jersey City, then connections were made for distant points. Railroad tracks in 1860 only went as far as Missouri. About two days later, Rarey's train puffed into the station at Columbus, Ohio. The exhilaration of being back must have chased off the chill of the December air as he travelled along that familiar ten-mile road to Groveport and his home.

And then came the joyful moments of seeing his mother Mary Catherine, and the well loved faces of his family, and introducing Cruiser, the mare and the quartet of ponies.

It was a merry Christmas this year, sharing dinner with his family, catching up on the news of who was doing what. How wonderful to look out again on the fields he had wandered over so many times, trying to discover the secrets of horses, as they grazed, played and battled in the meadows.

The visit, alas, was a short one. For the tour of the eastern cities was set to begin in the first week of January. Boarding the train, Rarey, Cruiser, and a duo of ponies – Gyp and Prince, were on the road again.

Rarey's entrance into New York was not noted in the papers, but somebody else's was. *Frank Leslie's Illustrated Newspaper* mentioned rather belatedly on 14 January: 'Among the distinguished artists lately arrived, we must not forget to record, was Cruiser, the famous horse tamed by Mr Rarey. He came by the Cornelius Grinneil. We are surprised that the City Hall has not been tendered to him as a reception room.'

Obviously not everyone was pleased with all the commotion surrounding Rarey and Cruiser. One person who specialized in commotion though, was anxious to meet Rarey – the showman P. T. Barnum. During 1858–9, Barnum had been in England lecturing on 'The Art of Making Money', so it's odd they hadn't met before. He sent the following letter on his American Museum stationery, with a little picture of the building on it, on 3 January 1861.

My Dear Rarey,

I am sorry I can't get a peek at you. Do please drop in occasionally till I can get the pleasure of shaking you by the hand. Have Fillingham's ponies arrived? If so, where are they?

Truly Yours,

P. T. Barnum

Barnum had an agent in London, Robert Fillingham. In the past, Barnum had ordered miniature ponies from London, to pull a tiny carriage for Tom Thumb, the 32-inch man who had toured the world over with Barnum. At his museum, Barnum currently had a new man of small stature, entertaining crowds, named George Washington Morrison McNutt, or as Barnum billed him Commodore Nutt. He was eighteen years old, twenty-nine inches tall and weighed twenty-four pounds.

In London, the agent Fillingham perhaps had sent some ponies over in the same ship as Rarey's Shetlands. Fillingham's little horses may have been a mystery, but Rarey's Gyp and Prince were in town, ready to perform 'comicalities of all kinds', at their first performance on Saturday 5 January at 3 o'clock.

The papers announced on Saturday that a violent horse named Joe Anderson, ironically the same name as the horseman in Piccadilly, was on his way to the show.

> Mischievous treatment in early horsehood soured the natural sweetness of his disposition, and from the time an accidental injury was inflicted on him with a pitchfork, he has never been known to do a kindly thing...His owner Mr Luff, a hosteler of high fame in the up-town eastern side of the city, is incredulous of Mr Rarey's powers and will be satisfied if the redoubtable Joe can be subdued, even with the grim hand of death. Doors open at 2 o'clock.
>
> New York Times

The doors opened upon an incredible mob scene of people pushing and shoving to get in. The *New York Times* published an article on 7 January which gives a colourful detailed eye-witness account of what it was like to sit at the ringside of Rarey's 'Exposition on Horsemanship'. When the curtain bell rang

> The curtain was rolled up and a well arranged Stable-Yard with boarded sides and rear, a roped front, and a sawdusted ground was disclosed to the view. Upon the sawdust was heaped hay to the depth of 12 to 14 inches. Into this area, Mr Rarey advanced on a long dog-trot, until he

reached the centre, when he stopped and spoke as follows:

'Ladies and Gentlemen – It will afford me pleasure in my lecture this afternoon to explain to you the peculiarities in my system of horse-taming...I have but recently returned from England...where it was publicly stated that what I had done was all very well, but that there was one horse I wouldn't dare to touch...[he gave a brief history of Cruiser then continued] I will now present for your consideration, Cruiser.'

Out bounded the far-famed animal – fire in his eye, blood in his nostrils, nerve in his ear, and pride in his port. Not so lithe of limb as we expected to have seen, but a stallion of undisputed blood, a descendant of noble sires, and only degraded in the odious squaring of his long and bushy tail. Curiosity is an undoubted element in

Portrait of Rarey and Cruiser, by Miner Kellogg, painted in 1860
(Collection of the Ohio Historical Society)

Cruiser's character. He looked knowingly up and down, to the right and the left, and, as if pleased by the immensity of his audience and the thunderous applause there from, neighed most spiritedly, and fondled Rarey with his head.

Mr Rarey then stated that Cruiser had not been on the stage since he left England, and had no rehearsal, and was as fresh to him as to the audience, 'yet', said he, 'instead of kicking and pulling as he used to do, he will fondle me with his head and give me his foot like a gentleman'– both of which things he then did. Rarey and the horse then proceeded to walk up and down, they trotted briskly around the stage, they wheeled about and turned about and did every thing that equine or human muscle will permit of, until they wearied. Then the tamer took from his pocket two leather belts or straps...

Running his hand quietly down the left foreleg of the horse, Mr Rarey quickly fastened the strap about his fetlock, and pulling it up, removed from the horse one fourth of his motive capacity. He led him limping around the stage, the horse being unable to paw or strike out with his feet. He then fastened the second strap on the fetlock of the off fore-leg, and ran it through the belly-band. The horse was then started forward, the strap being pulled stringently at the same time, and in the twinkling of an eyeball, the animal was upon his knees. For a while he struggled but finally yielded, and fell upon his side. While in this position, Rarey jumped over him, crept about his legs, stood by him and gently stroked him; then taking him by the head, he pulled…, indicating Christian forebearance on the part of Cruiser.

All at once and unexpectedly, after the straps had been loosed, the horse leaped up and dashed wildly at an attendant, who, dressed in black with his arms folded, had been contemplating the performance in the attitude of Napoleon at Fontainbleau, causing him to jump into the air about eight feet, and then ran frantically around the area, until Mr Rarey caught Cruiser and explained to the audience that Cruiser's sides were quite sore from chafings received in the stall on shipboard, and consequently he did not like to be dragged about.

The audience generously gave several rounds of applause, during which Mr Rarey retired, taking the horse, once so wild and nervous but now so gentle and calm…

Having brushed his coat and his hair, Mr Rarey announced the second part of the entertainment to be a trial of his skill upon a large white horse, who, though generally tractable, was exceedingly nervous, and, according to the statement of the person who brought him, has so hard a mouth that he invariably 'pulls his owner's arms off'.

The horse was a fine appearing animal, of good action and powerful carriage, and during the remarks of Mr Rarey stood patiently by his side.

'The horse,' said Mr Rarey, 'has a mind as well as you or I. Every action is premeditated – every start, kick, shrinking, or running, is caused by fear or anger. He is influenced by outward surroundings as we are, and has his loves and his hates. The horse is the most noble of all animals – his nature is that of kindness to everyone, and only when he fears hurt or harm will he evince other than a good disposition. You can never tame a horse by brutal treatment – rough breaking does no good – but much harm. The first deed to be attained by a trainer is a thorough understanding between himself and his horse.'

'Never run at a horse. Most people attempting to catch a horse, grab at him thus' here suiting the action to the word, Mr Rarey rushed at the horse, who naturally jumped back. Rarey then feinted a grab at his bridle, which he also resisted…'That,' resumed the lecturer, 'is the popular way of catching a horse. How would you like it if, meeting a friend in the street, you should be caught by your nose? Not much. Well, the horse is just as sensitive about his nose as you are about yours.'

'Treat him kindly, use him gently, and you can handle his head with perfect impunity, and not only that, but he will rest it against you, and put his head in your pocket, if it's big enough.' (Here Mr Rarey smoothed, stroked, caressed and fondled the animal's head, and in a moment his nervous trepidation was gone – he was gentle, he was kind, and we think you'd rarely find a nicer horse than that old grey.)

'The trouble with this horse,' said Rarey, 'is that he pulls dreadfully. His owner says he can't hold him, and that he heads so strong as to pull the driver's arms off. Now there is no need of that. If you only understand the nature of the horse and impress upon him the stern but gentle fact of your mastery, he will not be fractious. He will obey a gentle pull quicker than a hard one. His mouth is very sensitive, you can't improve it. It is a well known fact that horses will obey a lady's guiding better than a man's – it is because they don't pull so hard.'

'Now this horse who pulls so hard, and whose driver is in constant fear of arm dislocation, I have never seen before, and yet I will, as now I do, lead him with a straw. It is the most natural thing in the world for a horse, when he finds you intend to subjugate him, to pit himself against you – to try strength against strength and will against will.' (Here, and during the latter part of these remarks, Rarey led the horse hither and thither by means of a straw, which he had looped through the bit ring.) It was like the old song of 'Mary had a little Lamb'…Hard puller or not, we cannot say, but one thing is certain, he obeyed perfectly, to the entire justification of the tamer, and the satisfaction of the audience, who manifested the same by a blistering clapping of hands, a dust raising stamping of feet, and a throat scraping torrent of 'Hi Hi Hi's' such as a New York sports alone can give, which caused the horse to start as if frightened.

'If,' continued Mr Rarey, 'the audience will kindly suppress any manifestation of applause I will consider it a favor, and will be able more easily to proceed with my operations.' Perfect silence indicated the willingness to oblige Mr Rarey who at once proceeded...'I have often,' said he, 'been angry with farriers for the way in which they took hold of a hoof when about to shoe it, grabbing it as if it was a roasted apple in a furnace. Begin thus – pat the horse's neck and shoulder, lean yourself familiarly against the upper part of his leg, then run your hand gently and soothingly down to his foot, then easily, steadily, take it up. All motive for resistance being absent, the foot will lie peacefully in your hand, the nerves are relaxed, and there will be no trouble.'

'Now I will, although there is no absolute necessity for it in this case, apply the straps, as on Cruiser, and you will see the same results. There, now, the strap is on and the horse has learned his first lesson. Namely, that though he can walk, and so to speak trot, he is powerless for evil. This is a good way to use with horses who are ugly in harness. And by the way, I will here say a few words about the reasons which impel horses to kick when in harness.

They kick because they are afraid – looking back, they see the wheels running after them. They at once think – *for think they do* – that they ought to run too, and so they try it on; that being the case, the wheels keep up with the horse, and he, finding that he can't get away, becomes still more frightened, and begins to kick, and kicking gets hurt. The hurt continues his fear until the wagon is smashed to pieces. Now, if the horse had been shown the wagon, and nosed it, and been aware of its peaceful nature, he would not be afraid. If not, he will do the same every time he is put before a wagon, and if he is not always so bad, he will invariably have fear, just as you, who, having been bitten by a neighbor's savage dog, would never go by the house again without dreading a reoccurrence of the bite, and would keep a sharp lookout.'

The horse meanwhile had been standing on a tripod, doubtless wondering at the novel position in which he was placed and at the vast audience before him. Mr Rarey, having fastened the second strap, endeavored to trip the horse, but the horse was not inclined to be tripped...

Rarey with all his might held the strap, with all his might he pushed against the horse, but he didn't succeed...and not a few thought Rarey had met his match – but he wiped his face with his handkerchief and said: 'It is useless to be in a hurry – the difference between me and this horse is simply a difference of opinion, he thinks I can't get him down, and I think I can. After he has kicked and plunged a little longer – at the very longest 15 minutes, and has gotten himself and me too, entirely out of breath, he will be convinced...I, you see, am in no danger; the horse can't kick or paw me. I keep close by his shoulder and patiently wait.'

The horse at this point made one final struggle, gave one rousing farewell coup de two legs, and rolled over on his side...Rarey immediately went through a series of gymnastic performances such as he did with Cruiser, stroking and soothing the horse. He was in the act of undoing the second strap, when some graceless unbeliever in the second tier cried out, 'Say Pop, tell us how you got that strap on Cruiser, that's what we want to know.' At which about 1998 people, virtuously indignant, hissed, and two aiders and abettors of the scoffing inquisitor sustained him saying, 'Yes, tell us that – that's a very different thing?'

'I'll tell you about that at another time,' said Rarey.

'And that will cost another dollar, I suppose,' responded the 'voice' – who was instantly greeted with a second storm of hisses, after which little episode, and the proposal by some bloods to 'throw that fellow out.' Mr Rarey went on: 'This horse, upon whose back I am now sitting, is conscious that I do not intend to abuse my power, and is content as a forgiven child would be – (whereupon the horse keeled over with his hind legs and threw Rarey on the ground) – *That*, is because he isn't tamed all over; a horse may be tame in his forefeet and wild in his hind feet...'

In as much as the white horse was not 'tamed all over'...Rarey further stroked and smoothed him until he could handle his hooves as you would a knife and fork, so that no one could doubt the truth of his assertion, 'Now, the horse is tamed all over.' Continuing his address he said, 'There are a great many ways of harnessing and saddling horses. By some of them you can spoil the best tempered animal in the world. You can scare the life out of him, you can make him nervous, peevish and fretful. In this, as in everything, the basis on which you should work, is that the horse has common sense. If you put your hand before his eyes, if you go carefully behind him, he says to himself, 'That fellow's up to mischief.' But if you let him see that all is right, he doesn't care what you put on him. Now, for instance, I take this saddle (suiting the action to the words) and first of all show it to the horse. He smells it, looks at it carefully, and makes up his mind that it won't hurt, bite, or injure.

I then put it thus, over his head, down his neck, on to his back. He has seen it and doesn't object. In mounting a horse...you don't want to have all of your weight come on one side of the horse. If you do, the saddle is drawn on one side, and it is not easy for the horse to sustain it; but you should place your hand on his neck, bearing thereon so that the hand shall balance the foot, then spring lightly in…

In the head the horse has immense power. No man can ever hope to hold in a running horse by pulling evenly upon the bit; he might as well try to lift himself over a fence by pulling at his bootstraps. When a horse's head is turned to one side, he is compelled to so arrange his legs that they will properly balance him – he cannot run forward. Therefore, my advice would be if a horse is running away or if he refuses to go, to pull on one rein causing the horse to describe a circle.

They profit by experience, of which fact the old story of the donkey, who was laden with sacks of salt is an illustration. The donkey, by lying down in the water, melted the salt and eased his burden, so that he frequently repeated the experiment, until his master, preferring an upright donkey to a prone one, loaded him one day with bags of sand. Which, being wet by the donkey's trick, became so heavy that he could not rise, and never after did his lordship try the experiment.

As it is with the saddle or the harness, so it is with all other articles or even noises. Some horses are frightened by a band of music, and the noise of a drum sets them crazy. Now look at this horse, I hold the drum before him. He regards it most intelligently. Now I beat it gently, he pricks up his ears. I beat louder, he doesn't care. I let him see me place it upon his back, he doesn't mind. I beat like thunder, and he doesn't regard it as worthy of the least notice.

So, ladies and gentlemen, you have seen that this horse is entirely gentle…If you favor me with your patience, I will presently show you something of a different kind, which I have not seen myself, but which, I am told, promises me some hard work.' Mr Rarey here retired and the big horse with him, receiving as they went the most vociferous applause.

Shortly after, Mr Rarey reappeared, and stated that a wild horse from South America, which had never been broken except to the halter, would now be introduced. The doors opened, and it was evident from the noises, the kickings and stamping, that great fun would soon be afforded to the audience.

In rushed a little pony, with a long shaggy mane, a plump stubby body, a thick wag-tail, a very rough coat and unshodden hooves. Glaring at the audience, he planted his two fore feet firmly on the ground, and kicked his hinder legs high in the air, while his tail stuck straight out like a broom. Down he came towards the footlights, and rearing upon his hind legs, stood there erect, while he furiously pawed the air with fore legs, and seemed to bid defiance to Mr Rarey and the delighted audience, and dare them, one and all, to touch one single hair. Cautiously but firmly, Rarey advanced towards his little friend in brown and attempted to jump upon his back – he did it once, he did it twice, he did it three times; but was unable to get on, and the little chap neighed out a sneering horse laugh as he advised him to 'do so some more'. We all rejoiced in the spunk of the little chap...

We hoped he would prove game to the end, but our hopes were dashed and pony's doom was sealed, when Mr Rarey disclosed the straps. Having succeeded in arranging both straps, it became simply a question of time, as to the result. Pony didn't exactly understand at first – up in the air – down on the ground – now on this side – now on that – eyes flashing, with ears thrown forward and backward with great rapidity, with nostrils distended, and whisking tail did he try his power against that of inexorable fate. His will was tremendous, his determination complete.

On the other hand, it was a treat to watch the Tamer. His physical strength must be very great, and his power of endurance far beyond the average. He was entirely self-possessed, very careful, soothing, watchful, firm, patient and very un-relenting. The perspiration rolled in streams down his cheeks, and we no longer wondered why he had two handkerchiefs, one in his breast pocket and one in his coat-tail pocket. He needed them both. During the contest, he made occasional descriptive remarks, showing the why and wherefore, and explaining the reasons of every movement. Of course he conquered, he always does, it is his way.

The little horse, seeing that there was but one way to happiness, undoubtably made up his mind that this was a queer country, and that its people have strange ways towards animals, and peacefully surrendered. After a while, he was unstrapped, his heels were knocked together, the gymnastic experiments were gone through with, Mr Rarey jumped upon his back and from thence made a few remarks.

'Now,' said he, 'this little fellow...considers me his friend. If he didn't, he'd try to get away. He likes me, and will, as you see, follow me wherever I go. I will now show you my Shetland ponies, after which I will deter you but a short time.'

The exhibition of the two well formed but very diminutive Shetlands was the text for a brief discourse upon the cause of their size. Mr Rarey believes that they are sons of the Arab race, who, having for years been stinted in food, and enfeebled by inter-crossing, have become stunted in growth, though perfect in form...

The exhibition of Cruiser gratified the curiosity of many, the contest with the South American pony pleased the fancy of many; but the taming of a vicious biting horse, excited the liveliest interest and absorbed the entire attention of the audience in the most wonderful degree.

After announcing that he had received letters about several horses in the country, who had not yet arrived; Mr Rarey read the following, which was received with tumultuous applause, the writer being well known, and his horse enjoying a similar notoriety.

HARLEM LANE

Mr J. S. Rarey,

Having heard that you want vicious horses, I beg to inform you that I have a fine stallion which cost me $2,700 but he is so vicious I have been able to do nothing with him for four years…He has not been out of the stable, and cannot be shod. He is vicious in every way – biting, kicking, striking. I do not believe you can do anything with him, but if you wish, you can try.

Very Respectfully,
E. Luff

The horse was a stallion of great power and beauty. His carriage was noble, and his air that of a war horse 'who smelleth the battle from afar and who snorteth gaily at the sound of the trumpets'. Over his mouth was a heavy iron muzzle, and he was led in by two stable boys, who looked as if they were frightened and acted as if they expected to be hurt…The horse was particularly sensitive about his head, and his owner stated he would allow no one to touch him. When Rarey

Keeping the horse from biting
(*Frank Leslie's Illustrated Newspaper* 19 January 1861)

attempted to place gently his hand upon his face, he would snort and plunge in the most disgusted manner.

After he was down – after he had been thoroughly subjugated fore and aft...he allowed Mr Rarey to remove the muzzle and approach his head. The owner of the horse had cautioned Mr Rarey about letting him catch hold of him, saying that he would never let go; but to the utter surprise of everyone, Mr Rarey not only ran his hand through the horse's mouth, but allowed his naked hand to remain there for some time...

'Now,' said Rarey, 'I don't fear that any harm will come to me. I have tamed horses, and advertised to do so, since I was 12 years old. I have had almost every limb and many bones of my body broken, but being healthy they have healed, and I stand as firm on my legs as ever.

I renew my challenge to the world: I will take every and any horse that can be brought to me and will tame and gentle him by this method. I propose to give another entertainment on Tuesday next. I thank you for your cheering presence and your kind attention...'

Mr Rarey then retired, while the audience testified their admiration of his skill and their satisfaction with his entertainment, in their hearty and enthusiastic manner. Again Mr Rarey appeared – again he bowed, and again he retired, covered with sawdust and glory.

His motto is a good one, and none the worse for its antiquity or its source. We take pleasure in presenting it in full to our readers: 'A Merciful Man is Merciful to his Beast.'

13

A NEVER-GIVE-UP GREY

HINGS went wrong at the second performance on Tuesday 8 January at the very start. A crush of people created pandemonium by rushing in and taking over the reserved seat sections. Rarey apologized during the show, stating that reserved ticket holders could exchange their seats for Thursday's performance or get their money back; but it was so noisy that practically no one heard him say it.

Theatre patrons at Niblo's were known to be lively. Top hats parked in the aisles were often used for target practice, and the orchestra pit was steadily rained upon by flying missiles from the gallery. Rarey's lecture ran along the same lines as before, but none of the horses exhibited the flash and fury of the first time, so many came away disappointed. After the show, to smooth ruffled feathers, Rarey sent a letter to the *New York Times*:

> A CARD TO THE PUBLIC
> Metropolitan Hotel
> Tuesday evening Jan. 8

I greatly regret that by some mismanagement more tickets were sold for my lecture this evening than the capacity of the house would justify, and many reserved seats were taken possession of by those who were not entitled to them. I wish to inform the public it was done without my knowledge or sanction, and I promise that such an occurrence shall not take place again.

> Very Respectfully,
> John S. Rarey

In the volatile see-saw of public opinion, Rarey emerged on the upswing with his next performance, and so did his partner. The *New York Times* on 11 January related:

Cruiser appeared to be in better humour than usual, and did all that was required of him with excellent grace, following his master like a huge Newfoundland dog, and even condescending to carry a small parcel between his teeth – those puissant teeth – which, in days of yore, were the terror of stable-boys and hope of surgeons.

Harper's Weekly, 19 January 1861,
'Cruiser is becoming rapidly Americanized.
Naturally enough, he takes to straw drinks.'

After Cruiser had trotted off, a black mare was introduced and while with her, Mr Rarey… said that he did not wish to appear before the public in the character of a gladiator merely to fight wild beasts, but rather as an educator; the exponent of a system which he knew to be correct and which he desired to promulgate for the good it could do…He is one of those men who never seem to be in the way, but stand always where they should stand, calmly, and ready for action. A more unruffled person could hardly be found in the auditorium, and certainly not another to convey the idea of the hand of iron in the glove of silk more completely.

The influence of his lectures extended beyond the horse world, for editorials appeared suggesting that his method be used to gentle the warring factions tearing the country in two. At this point, seven states had seceded from the Union.

'Mr Rarey has arrived at an opportune moment', the *New York Times* wrote in January, 'If there is no vacancy at present in the Cabinet, one should speedily be made for him. Our Executive might borrow some important hints from him in the art of government.'

President-Elect Lincoln was still living in Springfield, Illinois. He was scheduled to take office on 4 March. His wife, Mary Todd Lincoln, was in New York on 14 January, a bitterly cold 10-degree day, shopping for fashionable furnishings for the White House. Across town, Edwin Booth was starring in a play by Shakespeare, at the New Bowery Theatre. Their names would be painfully linked in future days when Booth's brother John Wilkes Booth would play a role in the crime of the century.

Over the next two weeks, Rarey gave performances on 12, 15 and 17 January and on Saturday the 19th. The advertisements for the 19th stated that the 'beautiful and celebrated trotting mare Flora Temple will be shown to the audience'. There was a keen interest among horse people in seeing the famed 'trotting cracks' of the day. Introducing notable horses such as Flora Temple helped to perk up interest and keep the people coming in.

Rarey's publicity was well orchestrated, with large ads appearing in the newspapers several days beforehand. A business manager or advance agent would have taken care of this. The agent would also secure the theatres, arrange for transportation and lodging, plus find stabling for Cruiser and the ponies.

A man named W. B. Barton acted as Rarey's advance agent, for on 18 January he was in Philadelphia negotiating with the Board of Directors Executive Committee to lease the Academy of Music. The cost for leasing the beautiful opera house for three nights in February was $450, payable in advance. The agreement made, the acoustics there would soon be tested by the echo of a new sound – the neighing of horses instead of the singing of opera stars.

Back in New York, Rarey's Farewell Exhibition was set for Saturday 26 January at 2.30. Snow and ice coated the city, but Niblo's was filled to the rafters. The *New York Times* on 28 January reported that:

> Mr Rarey began as usual with Cruiser. Cruiser is worth a mint of money to Rarey. He is Rarey's big thing. On no occasion do the public weary of him, they love to hear all about him; what Lord Dorchester said, what Rarey said, and then what Dorchester said back again.
>
> Cruiser was very happy, and apparently pleased with himself and his audience, for after doing all he was told by Rarey, he volunteered several high and mighty performances on his own account, which showed he

still felt his oats, and considered himself as much a man and brother as anybody.

The first horse introduced had only been ridden once and had shown her owner, 'what goes up must come down'. She was 'unaccustomed to the rein, but soon by line upon line, by little deeds of kindness and little words of love, Rarey taught her the way in which she should go, and rode her with perfect safety all around the ring'.

The last horse on the programme, a cast-iron grey with the will power to match, was not so easily convinced. A big, powerful looking horse with a long mane and tail, he was 'not particularly bad', said his owner, 'that is he never killed anybody, but he is absolutely unmanageable'.

The *New York Times* related:
At first Rarey patted him, soothed him, and stroked him. Then he slid his hand down to his hoof and attempted to buckle the strap around the joint. For some time he was unsuccessful, but finally got it. The next attempt was to fasten the foreleg up.

Rarey taking up the foreleg
(*Frank Leslie's* 19 January 1861)

This Mr Rarey usually accomplishes in half a minute, but on this occasion he was delayed at least an hour and a quarter. Time and time and time again did he almost accomplish his purpose, but time and time again was he foiled. It was evident that the horse knew what he was about – what his opponent was trying to do. Several times Rarey succeeded in getting the strap around the leg, and the end of it through the buckle, but before it could be fastened, the foot would go with terrific force to the ground, destroying in a second the work of many minutes.

At one time it was done, the buckle was fastened, and all seemed secure, when with an immense effort, the horse by his muscular power snapped the strap as if it had been a straw and stood quietly free again!

Gradually the horse became excited, then angry and finally frantic, while Rarey, whose pluck and strength are apparently superhuman, worked patiently to the end. It seemed to the spectator as if Rarey must be in great danger, as whenever the horse made the effort to free his leg, he would start violently forward.

On one occasion while Rarey was bending over the knee, the horse rushed forward, throwing him far out towards the centre of the ring, and then pranced proudly about the enclosure. Again, when his head was fastened by a leather halter to a fence, he snorted loudly, pulled quickly, and breaking the strap, jerked the bridle from his head, sprang over the crouching form of his opponent, and ran around the ring as if attempting to jump over.

This caused a half-suppressed exclamation of horror all over the house; the ladies occupying the front seats insisted upon going elsewhere, and one pious-looking gentleman with long hair, green spectacles and black gloves said, in agitated tones, 'I would like to ask Mr Rarey if there is any danger of the horse's doing injury to those in the dress circle.' Whereupon a series of cat calls, dry-ups and laughter squelched him, put the audience in good humor, and still further frightened the horse.

At this time, say three quarters of an hour after the struggle began the contestants were a sight to behold. Rarey's hair was – well, not to be particular, messy; his face was red, and his clothes were sawdust from 'the nape of his neck to the slack of his breeches'; while the horse was in a completely perspiratory state. The water ran from him in streams as if he had been ducked in the North River...He didn't care a 'continental cuss' for Rarey, for the audience...or for the fact that 5 o'clock is the universal dining hour of Christians and metropolitans...

How in the name of the ancient gladiators – how in the name of muscle – Rarey was able to endure is more than we can understand... After further struggles of a similar nature, Rarey succeeded in running the strap through the surcingle...but not until repeated efforts had proved unavailing. At last – and that at last always comes, he securely adjusted the straps, and then of course the game was up.

The horse was soon down, handled, quieted and caressed. His spirit was not tamed, his fire and strength remained, for he acquiesced

Through the surcingle
(*Frank Leslie's* 19 January 1861)

cheerfully in whatever was required of him, to the astonishment and delight of all.

After apologizing for the delay – stating that it was owing to the breaking of the strap, and the fact that he was in too much of a hurry – Mr Rarey thanked the audience for their patronage and attention, and announced that on Saturday next, he will give an entertainment [with half the proceeds] to benefit the Widows and Orphans Fund...

On Saturday 2 February, a dense fog blanketed the city. The streets were a sloppy sea of slush but it didn't deter the ticket-holders from Rarey's charity matinee in Brooklyn at the Academy of Music. Some 5,000 people watched and listened as Rarey told the long version of Cruiser's transformation, while the dark stallion stood beside him.

He then led away, as the *New York Times* said on 4 February, 'the horse in which all England, from Queen to cobbler, at one time felt a great interest; and who though tamed, and led quietly on and off stage, is kept from biting strangers by a wooden roller strapped firmly between his teeth'....

Later on, two horses were brought out that Rarey had met before – in Syria. These were the Arabian stallions given by Ayoub Bey to William H. Seward, who was soon to be nominated to Lincoln's cabinet. The horses were feisty, and one of the stallions was described by his groom as 'the best boxer he ever saw'.

Seward's Arabians
(*Harper's Weekly* 12 January 1861)

After a while the Shetlands were brought out and 'the larger pony rolled upon the straw and the little fellow, stood upon a tripod formed of his two hind legs and his tail'.

The programme was a full one, Rarey having handled several tough horses, but the worst was yet to come. On the stage appeared a horse named Peacock belonging to the Hudson River Railroad Company. Rarey managed to dodge his plunging, biting and kicking, then sprang on the horse's back.

Rarey riding
(*Frank Leslie's* 19 January 1861)

The *New York Times* wrote:

Rarey was thrown heavily to the ground – again and again was this attempted with the same result. The animal was thoroughly angry...and his tail, which is a mere switch, and by no means a proper appendage for a Peacock, wiggled with briskness from one side to the other. It being evident that his first lesson was not productive of any good result, Mr Rarey with exemplary patience, re-strapped him and finally succeeded in getting on him with safety, in playing with his heels, in soothing him from nose to tail to his heart's content. The performance being over, Mr Rarey announced his immediate departure for Philadelphia...

14

PHILADELPHIA, BALTIMORE, AND KICKING KATE

*T*HE temperature in Pennsylvania was bone-chillingly cold. Regardless, the city railways were full, and cabs and private carriages were trotting along in the streets of Philadelphia, on Tuesday 5 February. They were busy bringing about 3,000 shivering people to the opera house on Broad Street.

Inside, the Academy of Music was warm, heated by steam. The people in elegant evening dress took their seats, their way illumined by the glow of a huge sparkling chandelier. At 8 pm, the stableyard on stage was drawn back in the centre to make a passageway, and then a man dressed in black walked with a quick step to the footlights. A wave of applause rippled as he smiled and tipped his top hat.

John Rarey took a deep breath and began to address the audience: 'I am here for the purpose of showing my system of horse taming, mild yet firm, which does away with all rough breaking...'

After the entrance and exit of Cruiser, he worked with a nervous bay horse. In the midst of this he stated that the best way to deal with nervousness was to 'make a firm impression upon him that you could do what you pleased, but that you did not intend to hurt him'.

When Rarey was finished handling this horse and led it away, he returned carrying something in his arms. The audience could just make out the outline of a little head bobbing as he walked. As he came into the light, the mystery creature was revealed to be Gyp, his 77-pound Shetland pony. His other pony Prince came trotting out alongside him, and stood by as he talked about their origin and size.

The next horse to take the stage was a bay mare from 7th Street, who had been blacklisted by farriers after her first shoeing. Only one farrier would work on her now, if her legs were tied together. She had been ridden but once, for she 'cut up such capers they thought it prudent' not to try again. Her name was Kicking Kate.

Rarey came up to her quietly and ran his hand over her back. 'She immediately vindicated her name', the *Philadelphia Inquirer* noted on 6 February, 'by kicking repeatedly and savagely, to the great amusement of the audience who could not help laughing though Mr Rarey had previously asked for silence'.

After an encounter of the strapping kind and then the soothing and stroking, Kate relinquished her kicking. Soon he was handling all her legs, even placing his head against her hoofs. 'He remarked in closing', said the *Inquirer*, 'he was willing to undertake any horse, just as he had Kate...'

This was no empty showman's promise. In all the places he'd been, no matter how dangerous the horse, he had never backed down; such was the utter faith he had in his method and his understanding of horses.

Another capacity crowd braved the biting cold on Thursday 7 February, to attend his second lecture. An icy wind was whipping through town, 'unroofing houses' and toppling chimneys. The north wind may have been stirring up the fire in Cruiser as well, for he made his entance looking 'more spirited than when he appeared on these boards on Tuesday night', the *Philadelphia Inquirer* wrote on 8 February. 'He pranced around the stage quite lively, and kicked a quantity of tan over into the orchestra pit among the reporters.' [Tan was oak or other bark having tannin, used in tanning leather. The leftovers were spread in circus rings.]

Another crowd pleaser came on next, in the form of Kicking Kate. Rarey brought her back to demonstrate that a saddle could now be put on her 'with ease if gentle treatment were used'. He went through the steps of introducing her to the saddle, letting her see and sniff it, and eventually was riding her without any problems.

Trouble was not far behind though, for a grey head with a pair of long ears was waiting in the wings. As Kicking Kate made her exit, a mule belonging to the Pennsylvania Railroad Company was

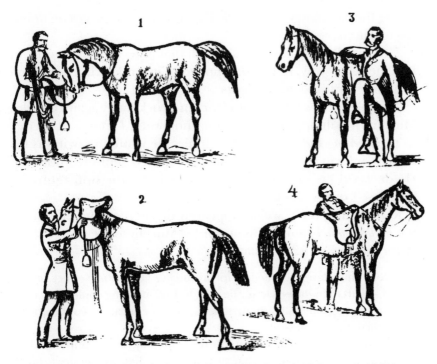

Introducing a horse to the saddle (*Frank Leslie's* 19 January 1861)

led blinking into the lights. Everything went rather well until Rarey asked the mule to rise up from the floor. The *Philadelphia Inquirer* tells us: 'The mule took an obstinate fit and refused to get up for at least five minutes, during which its Roman firmness created tremendous outbursts of laughter.' They must have been five long minutes for Rarey.

After the ponies pranced, a powerful bay horse named Turco charged onto the stage. He had a 'dark, fierce mane and a warlike aspect', and his head was weighed down with a heavy muzzle. He started striking at Rarey as soon as he approached, illustrating why he was considered unshoeable and unrideable. After a struggle, Rarey got the straps on, but Turco did not agree with the idea of lying down. He went on plunging and bounding for almost nine minutes. Finally when Turco lay down, Rarey took the muzzle off. The horse jumped up quick as a flash, and 'danced around on its hind feet and bit at him like a snapping turtle'. Rarey eluded the turtle dance, got the straps back on and returned him to the ground. After some time gentling, he was placing his hand in the horse's mouth. A little while later, he said goodnight to the crowd while riding the bay charger bareback. But that was not the last he would see of Turco.

The overflowing crowds showed that interest was strong in Philadelphia, so W. B. Barton applied to extend their lease of the Academy for three more nights.

The following week, public criticism struck Rarey again. Charles Murphy of Wilmington, Delaware, who owned Turco, sent a letter to the *Evening Bulletin* in Philadelphia. He wrote to say it was his right to inform the public that Rarey had accomplished nothing. He declared he was downright disgusted with the swift return of his horse's disagreeable habits.

Rarey sent a reply, which appeared in the morning edition of the *Philadelphia Inquirer*. This prompted Murphy to fire off a rebuttal to the *Inquirer* on 12 February:

> I deny that Rarey succeeded in producing any lasting effect on my horse Turco. In Rarey's letter he says: 'I think nothing could be plainer than my repeated statement that a horse's education could not be perfected in one lesson...
>
> Turco has been handled in just the same way before, and it had no lasting effect on him. He has now been handled by the great horse tamer of the world, and he is a much wickeder horse than ever, without, as Mr Rarey says, being teased in his stall...Mr Rarey says he was not hurried off the stage through fear, but being the last subject, it is the usual course. Such may be his programme, but if I had known that would be the finale of his performance with Turco, I should not have sent him so far, for so little benefit... Mr Rarey says if I will send my horse back on Thursday evening, that he will show me that he can accomplish all that he wishes. He should have thought of that when my horse was in Philadelphia...As to sending Turco again, I beg to be excused, as I have not the time to spare, even should I have the faith; neither do I think I would be justified in incurring the expense for Mr Rarey's aggrandizement.

Whether Mr Murphy changed his mind or was coerced by friends isn't clear, but on St Valentine's Day, Turco was backstage at the Academy. The *Philadelphia Inquirer* commented on 15 February:

> The recent doubts of Mr Murphy – and the fact that Turco was again to be put on trial, made the occasion unusually interesting...Mr Rarey said that he did not propose to finish the education of a vicious horse in one lesson. In a week or fortnight he could however, tame the worst specimen of the equine race.

After the first horse was handled:

> Turco was then introduced and his subjugation was a difficult feat. Mr
> Rarey was successful in the end, and retired among the warm plaudits
> of the audience. Then there was a general cry for Mr Murphy to which
> that gentleman responded by coming upon the stage and briefly saying,
> 'I am perfectly satisfied.'

But others still had bones to pick. Rarey was brought to task in
various letters published in Philadelphia papers. There were charges
that he was taking undue credit for everything he spoke about,
such as the ways of mounting and saddling horses.

The editors of the *Philadelphia Inquirer* recognized this wasn't
the case and wrote in the 16 February edition: 'It is only fair towards
Mr Rarey to say that we have not understood him to claim he is the
discoverer of his mode of turning a horse, or of mounting one…Mr
Rarey on the contrary, disclaimed any merit of his own with respect
to several of his processes.'

An anonymous letter-writer from West Philadelphia believed that
Rarey's only original point and most helpful contribution was of
strapping the forelegs to lay the horse down.

His views, published on 16 February in the *Philadelphia Inquirer*,
stated that he believed Rarey's method conformed

> to the horse's natural method of laying down…The old way using straps
> from the shoulders to the fetlocks of the hind legs, was objectionable
> and dangerous. It often strained the loins of the horse, dislocated his
> hips, broke his ribs, ruptured him, or otherwise injured him…It excited
> a panic in the horse's mind. He is thrown off his feet in an unnatural
> way, which he will instinctively resist and dread…Roughness creates
> resistance. The horse means to do right, but does not always know
> how, and it is man's business to teach him with gentleness.

Rarey gave a final charity performance on Saturday 16 February,
with half the proceeds to be split among the various soup kitchens
in the city. Admission was one dollar for the Parquet, Parquet Circle
and Balcony, and the rest of the house was fifty cents.

The following morning, Rarey came down the lift of the
Continental Hotel at 9th and Chestnut Street, walked across the
black and white checkerboard floor in the lobby and checked out.
He boarded the train with Cruiser and the ponies, a train bound
for Baltimore, Maryland.

CONTINENTAL HOTEL, PHILADEL-
phia, February 14, 1861.
*To the Presidents of the various Soup Societies of Phila-
delphia:*

GENTLEMEN :—Having at my disposal an evening in Philadelphia previous to my departure for Baltimore, I have
determined to appropriate one-half the net proceeds of a
lecture on Saturday evening to the benevolent purposes
of the various societies represented by you. In order that
the amount, thus accruing may be apportioned among
you, pro rata—in proportion to the extent of your respective fields of operations—I propose to place it in the hands
of his Honor, the Mayor of this city, who has kindly consented to distribute it.

Respectfully, yours,   JOHN S. RAREY.

PHILADELPHIA. February, 14, 1861.
DEAR SIR :—Your considerate offer of a lecture, of which
one half the proceeds are tendered to us, as Presidents of
the various Soup Societies of Philadelphia, is a timely offering, which, on behalf of the suffering poor of this city,
we acknowledge and accept with sincere gratitude.

We recognize the judiciousness of the proposed appor-
tionment through the hands of his honor the Mayor, and
are   Yours, most respectfully,

JACOB T. BUNTING,
President of Society for Supplying the Poor with Soup,
   Griscom street.   CHARLES J. SUTTER,
President Northern Soup Society.
H. P. EYRE,
President of Kensington Soup Society.
L. B. M. DOLBY,
President Southwark Soup Society.
CHARLES RHOADES,
President Moyamensing Soup Society.
JAMES PETERS,
President Spring Garden Soup Society.

AMERICAN ACADEMY OF MUSIC,
In accordance with the above.
JOHN S. RAREY
Will give a charity lecture and exhibition of
HORSE TAMING,
Saturday evening, February 16th, at half-past seven.
One half the net proceeds of this lecture, will be distri-
buted among the various Soup Societies of this city, in
proportion to the extent of their respective fields of opera-
tions.

His Honor, Mayor HENRY, has kindly consented to act
as distributor.

These Societies are daily providing thousands with the
necessaries of life, and many of them are sadly in need of
funds.

Every effort will be made to render this among the
most interesting of Mr. Rarey's lectures.

Several vicious subjects have been secured for its practical illustration.

"Cruiser," and the smallest Shetland ponies in the
world will be exhibited.

ADMISSION.
Parquet, Parquet Circle, and Balcony................$1·00
All the rest of the house.................................... 50
The sale of tickets for Mr. Rarey's charity lecture will
commence this morning at the office of the Academy.

Letter in the *Philadelphia Inquirer*, 15 February 1861

As Rarey was leaving Philadelphia, someone of note was on his way, who would also stay at the Continental Hotel – President-Elect Lincoln. He was en route to Washington DC for the inauguration, making whistle stops at towns along the way.

On Thursday 21 February, Lincoln arrived in Philadelphia where a 'cavalcade of citizens escorted him through the city'. He gave an impromptu speech from the balcony of the Continental Hotel to a huge crowd in the street below, emphasizing that 'there is no need of bloodshed and war'.

Unfortunately, there were plenty of people ready to shed his blood. A plot was uncovered in Pennysylvania by detective Alan Pinkerton, that an assassination attempt was going to be made on Lincoln as the train was en route to Baltimore. After hearing the details, which included sabotage of a railroad bridge, and if that failed, grenades, pistols and daggers at the Baltimore station, Lincoln reluctantly agreed to go directly to Washington. He took an unmarked train, passing through Baltimore at night, and arrived safely in Washington on 23 February.

The press raked him over the coals for the incident, making it out to be an act of cowardice. Lincoln had continually to withstand their barbs in print. He was referred to as everything from a gorilla to a sandhill crane. They even pointed their spears at his 320-pound campaign manager Judge David Davis, who was, they said, 'so fat he had to be surveyed for a pair of pants'.

Bulk was one thing Rarey didn't have to worry about. 'A lithe, well-formed and closely knit figure' was how the *Baltimore American and Commercial Daily Advertizer* described him when he appeared at the Front Street Theatre on 19 February. And a chestnut stallion there also illustrated how he kept so thin.

This stallion 'protesteth much' and after his forelegs were bound, he practically ran upon his hind legs dragging Rarey, as the *Baltimore American* reported, 'around the ring to the imminent danger of his limbs, snapping and biting at him most vicously...and both the lecturer and the resisting subject were perspiring freely under the violence of their exertions'.

Later on, he spoke about another type of violence which many people could identify with and bears repeating: 'There is no more reason for the violent breaking of a horse than the violent breaking of a child. In either case, more can be accomplished by the hand of gentleness than by any method of force which human ingenuity

Bound but determined (*Frank Leslie's* 19 January 1861)

has yet devised.'

An educator in 1839 had echoed this thought, saying, 'The idea that difficulty in understanding or unwillingness to learn can best be cured by hitting a child with a stick is as stupid as it is degrading.'

Many families attended Rarey's show, for the whole family could watch without boredom or embarrassment. His business manager encouraged this in the advertisements. The matinee for 21 February was scheduled, it said in the advertisements, 'in order to particularly accommodate Ladies, Families, and Parties residing at a distance, the performance will close in time for all the afternoon trains.' Another item which spoke of an attitude now sadly gone was: 'Ladies may rely upon every attention being paid to their comfort.' But what this attention was – who knows!

Rarey's final appearance in Baltimore was on Saturday 23 February at 7.30. The tickets for the upper gallery were reduced to 25 cents, 'to give coachmen, hostelers, and all those who have the care and management of horses an opportunity to witness this last lecture'.

Like the cabmen in London, the hostelers and coachmen in America were on the low end of the pay scale. The average for wages was 25 to 50 cents a day. Most travelling circuses charged 25 cents admission, but to go to a 'Grand Calico Fancy Dress

Masquerade Ball' would cost a dollar.

In the midst of the uneasy early months of 1861, people were trying to carry on with dances, lectures, and everyday life, but these weren't normal times. The great topic on everyone's mind was the explosive unrest all over the nation.

A Commissioner from South Carolina, Mr Preston, declared in February at the Virginia Convention that his state 'had exercised the right of secession and was prepared for resistance to death...No sanctity of human touch would reunite the people of the North and the South.' The loud crack in the Union was also sending shock waves to the countries connected to her by bonds of friendship or commerce, like England. Queen Victoria, upon opening Parliament on 4 February mentioned: 'the troubles in America, expressing the fervent wish that an amicable adjustment might be attained'. But with each day dawning, the drumbeat of war sounded louder and louder. The bitterness was running as deep and black as the editorial in an Atlanta, Georgia newspaper:

> Let the consequences be what they may – whether the Potomac is crimsoned in human gore, and Pennsylvania Avenue is paved ten fathoms deep with mangled bodies or whether the last vestige of liberty is swept from the face of the American continent, the South will never submit to such humiliation and degradation as the inauguration of Abraham Lincoln.

The inauguration was now less than two weeks away.

15

BOIL, TOIL, AND TROUBLE

*I*NAUGURATION day, 4 March, dawned bleak, grey and cheerless, with a dripping of rain. Abraham Lincoln arose at 5 am determined to face whatever the day held for him – the presidency or a bullet. 'I anticipate no trouble', he had told his security force, 'but should it come, I am prepared to meet it.'

Throughout the night, a company of soldiers had guarded the wooden stand in front of the Capitol, after an informant reported a bomb was going to be placed underneath. As the morning hours passed, the weather cleared, and crowds gathered along the inaugural route.

At noon, Lincoln emerged from Willard's Hotel on 14th Street, into the sunshine. While a band played *Hail to the Chief*, Lincoln stepped into an open barouche carriage, joined by the white-haired out-going President James Buchanan. The moment was tense and they rode in silence. A square of militia and cavalry surrounded the carriage, the wind blowing dust in everyone's eyes. The horsemen were instructed to keep moving around the carriage, so no opportunity could arise for a clear shot.

As they proceeded along Pennsylvania Avenue, government sharpshooters watched from the rooftops. The streets were mobbed with about 30,000 on-lookers, but the crowd was strangely quiet. Arriving at the Capitol for the swearing-in ceremony, a battalion of troops stood at attention around the building, while riflemen lined the windows.

Lincoln and Buchanan enroute to the Inauguration
(*Harper's Weekly* 16 March 1861)

Lincoln ascended the stairs of the platform. After taking the oath of office, he delivered his address, calling for the country to stand as one. 'In your hands, my dissatisfied countrymen, and not in mine, is the momentous issue of civil war.' His closing statement echoed the deepest core of his goal for America:

> We are not enemies, but friends. We must not be enemies. Though passion may have strained, it must not break our bonds of affection. The mystic chords of memory, stretching from every battlefield, and patriot grave, to every living heart and hearthstone, all over this broad land, will yet swell the chorus of the Union, when again touched, as surely they will be, by the better angels of our nature.

Lincoln descended the platform and to the relief of all, no shots rang out. The headlines the following day declared, 'All's Well', and everyone knew what that meant.

In this volatile month of March 1861, was John S. Rarey among the crowds at the inauguration? The probability would point towards a yes, since he was in Washington DC at the end of February and early March. The *New York Times* ran an article, 'Rarey at Washington', on its front page on Tuesday 26 February, reporting that he was giving his first lecture on the evening of 27 February, 'in a building which he is having erected for the purpose at a cost of 1,000 dollars'.

A cynical article was published the next day, the writer seemingly offended by the carnival atmosphere among the vendors in the city. In the peculiar paragraphs, the writer took occasion to take a jab at Rarey.

> The Capitol is obstructed by peddlers of apples, ciders, boiled eggs – wonderful somebodies with wonderful somethings, their exhibition of which attracts a motley crowd. The latest contribution to these collections consists of a couple of coffins displayed in the old Hall of Representatives, perhaps to remind the politically dead of their coming fate.
>
> Rarey was compelled to erect a building especially for his exhibitions here. It is a wonder that he did not make successful applications for the use of the 'coffin-ware-room' which certainly is admirably adapted for his purposes, if he can teach his four-footed subjects to walk up the stairs.

The horses didn't go up the stairs, but did Rarey step into the White House to meet the new President? The daily report on Lincoln's day-to-day visitors in the White House during March does not include Rarey's name, but there may have been a private meeting. On 6 March, Lincoln was welcoming delegates from Ohio, such as Salmon P. Chase, the former governor of Ohio who had written a letter of recommendation for Rarey back in 1857 before he left for England.

Rarey had made the acquaintance of practically every royal head of the kingdoms and countries of Europe, and it follows that he would be introduced to the chief executive of his own country. Lincoln too, held a great appreciation for animals, and spoke fondly of his favourite horse which he had to leave behind in Illinois. This was a twelve-year-old bay gelding with ample belly named Old Bob.

Abraham Lincoln (centre) Salmon P. Chase (left)
William H. Seward (right) (*Harper's Weekly* 13 July 1861)

On the second of March, Rarey gave another performance in which a correspondent described the event as 'Rarey Meets a Second Cruiser – a severe contest with a kicking horse.' After this, there's no further mention of any of his exhibitions, but it seems logical he would have given a few more to cover the expense of the 1,000 dollar building.

By the latter half of March, however, he was on his way again; for the first week of April, Rarey and his retinue were in Massachusetts. Cruiser could now say neigh to Boston, and Rarey had the chance to meet William Lloyd Garrison, the fiery editor of *The Liberator*, a newspaper dedicated to exposing the cruelty of slavery. Garrison had been in the abolition movement since 1833.

After their meeting, Garrison mentioned in a letter to Rarey, dated 5 April 1861, that he was 'much gratified at the brief interview had with you this forenoon, as it deepened my conviction of your fitness to teach...an everywhere needed lesson of humanity...(so that) men might learn to govern their own passions, and thus substitute the law of love for the spirit of brutality'.

Present at one of Rarey's lectures in Boston was Ralph Waldo Emerson, the writer, lecturer, and philosopher. Emerson lived in Concord, Massachusetts, the same town as his friend the brilliant writer Henry David Thoreau. Sadly, Thoreau was suffering during this time from tuberculosis.

Emerson though was in good health, and after attending Rarey's lecture remarked: 'What excuse have we after an exhibition of Mr

Cruiser and Rarey shaking hands
(*Harper's Magazine* April 1861)

Rarey's treatment of the horse, for the use of brute force? He has turned a new leaf in civilization…What novelty in his fundamental maxim that he who would deal with a horse must know neither fear nor anger! When I saw his performance I could not help thinking it was a sort of Aesop's Fable and suspecting he was a very sly satirist…'

Another famous writer from Concord, Louisa May Alcott, author of *Little Women*, may have attended Rarey's Boston lectures, for she makes a brief reference to the character Laurie, horse-taming and 'playing Rarey'.

The next stop on the tour was Albany, New York, and there a true satirist had his day writing the following article. It was published anonymously in the *New York Clipper* on 13 April 1861 and titled 'Making Fun of Mr Rarey':

A meeting of the hack drivers, stable boys, hostelers, and others who attended Mr Rarey's free exhibition was held on Tuesday in the loft of Messrs Hall and Bumpus' stable, in Bridle Street, to exchange their sentiments regarding the exhibition they had witnessed, and to state its effect upon them. A Mr Jarvie presided. After a vote of thanks to Mr Rarey had been offered and passed, George Snaffle stated that he had tried Mr Rarey's plan, and found it first rate. He had always been very hard on a horse, and beaten him severely, but now he knew he had done wrong. Every morning since he had heard Mr Rarey, his practice was, the first thing upon going into the stable, to throw his arms around his horse's neck and ask his forgiveness for all his former cruelty. The result was that the animal would draw twice as heavy a load, and not say a word against it.

Mr Linchpin stated, that since hearing Mr Rarey he had not indulged in any profane language to his horse, but had invariably used terms of gentleness, such as 'Be kind enough to go on' and 'Don't, please, stand here in the way', and had found the horse perform much more satisfactorarily...

Mr Whiffletree had but that day experienced the benefit of Mr Rarey's system. His horse became refractory and refused to draw a load consisting of five hogsheads of molasses, whereupon he strapped up one of his legs, and he lay down quietly in the slosh, permitting him to lay down by him, which he accordingly did, after which the horse got up and looked around as though asking his driver to put on another hogshead. Experiences were also given by Messrs Lash, Bitt, Blinders, and others. The meeting adjourned status quo.

The weekend in April when that article was published turned out to be monumental in the fate of America. Unfortunately the better angels of human nature had receded to the background, and the bubbling kettle of conflict boiled over.

The Confederate States of America, the seven states that had seceded from the Union, had been demanding the surrender of the government's Fort Sumter in Charleston, South Carolina. When the Union's Commanding Officer Major Robert Anderson refused, the bombardment began on Friday 12 April. Major Anderson's troops were ill-equipped to withstand such an attack and thirty-four hours later on Saturday, they surrendered the fort.

On Monday 15 April, the headlines shouted CIVIL WAR and President Lincoln called for 75,000 militia for a three-month term to defend the Union. Overnight, Washington DC became a city under siege, as soldiers poured into the city. Patriotic fever raged through the country, as people were swept up in the excitement of the long simmering clash of ideas suddenly bursting into a war.

Where was the place for horse training and messages of kindness in the midst of all this bloodthirsty fever? Like a wildly dividing and deadly cancer, intolerance and chaos spread in all directions.

In Albany, New York, where Rarey had just been, the young men who would not take the oath to become soldiers were forced to leave town wearing white feathers attached to their heads. Where did Rarey's loyalties lie? He believed that the Union must be saved. But how could he go on with his performances in the light of all that was happening? The majority of circuses continued with their shows. Some even were flying the Confederate flag in the South and the American flag in the North.

Dan Rice, the talented clown and circus man, opened the 1861 season in Washington DC, then travelled north playing stands in Pennsylvania and Ohio. In Cincinnati, Ohio, an angry crowd demanded he raise a Union flag instead of the circus flag. He answered by pointing a howitzer at them, like an 1861 version of Clint Eastwood's 'Make My Day'.

Other circus men, like Old John Robinson in Cincinnati advertised: 'Southern men, Southern women, Southern horses, Southern enterprise against the world.'

Rarey was back in his world, Ohio, by the end of April. It had been a dynamic but long four months. He planned to resume his lectures in the autumn, for everyone believed the war would be over by then.

In May, plans were set in motion for Cruiser's other career – as a stallion. John's nephew, Henry Rarey, arranged for the publicity and issued a folder dated 4 May 1861 saying:

> The celebrated horse, 'Cruiser', imported from England, by John S. Rarey, will stand this season at the old homestead, at Groveport, Ohio…Cruiser is a combination of the very finest blood of England. Those who wish to study the English Stud Book can trace his pedigree back to the best families of horses ever bred in that country…

Description
Cruiser is a Dark Bay, nearly 16 hands high, with black legs, black mane and tail. He is of fine length and built for strength and speed; he has much stronger limbs and much more bone than is common among racehorses, and breeds large, strong colts. His head, a specialty with

the Venison stock, a perfect model of beauty, and his colts all bear this
mark of the horse.

Terms to Cruiser
Fifty dollars, with the privilege of returning the same or any other mare
if not with foal. Mares from a distance will be taken care of. For further
particulars address –

HENRY W. RAREY
Groveport, Ohio

An insert in the folder titled 'Cruiser and his Stock' had a detailed
history of his family tree and their careers on the race course.
Information was given too about the foals he had sired at Rawcliffe
Stud. Three of them became quite successful on the turf: Rajah
Brooke, Medora, and 'the gallant gray – Rattlebone, a very stout
runner true to the family forte, who liked a distance'. At this time,
Rattlebone, who had just been sold by Thomas Parr, the man whom
Rarey bought the King of Oude from, was standing at stud at the
Althorpe Paddocks, where Cruiser had stood in 1860.

The page concluded with: 'And thus it will not be on the Banks
of the Ohio alone, that the blood of Cruiser, Mr. Rarey's "Man
Friday" of three London seasons, will be spread in future years.'

But Cruiser did not stand alone. Also offered for stud were three
other horses. The first was 'Hopeful' an imported English Carriage
Horse of Cleveland Bay stock. 'Hopeful stands 16.1 hands, is a good
bay with black legs, and is a sure foal-getter and free of all blemishes',
the folder stated.

Next on the list was 'an imported Shetland Pony, jet black color,
superior form and action'; and then a trotting horse named
'Bellfounder'. The terms for these horses and the pony were ten
dollars.

As May and June slid by, the armies for both sides were drilling.
Recruitment posters calling men to arms were tacked up on posts
and in store windows in every village. Troops marched off to war in
pride and glory with cheering parades, and the bands played on.
The smell of the coming conflict was stirring heady excitement
among the young men and boys. The recruitment call was also
being put forth to another class of innocents – horses.

Massive numbers of horses were needed to move the army. Heavy
horses to pull the supply wagons, caissons or ammunition wagons,

and cannons; and lighter horses for the cavalry. Southern horsemen, though, laughed at the horses being mustered for the North, saying they were 'wide as a barn door and slow as molasses'.

By July, the armies were marching in the sultry heat of summer in Virginia. On the road, men collapsed with sunstroke, while others bled from the ears, nose and mouth from the heat and exhaustion.

Finally on 21 July, in the drizzling rain, the armies of the North and the South clashed head on near Manassas Junction in Virginia, by a stream called Bull Run. The months of pent up tension and anticipation exploded into a wild chaos of bursting artillery and brutal hand to hand combat. After the battle a panic broke out, a 'shouting and screaming mass of men'. In one horrible day, war had lost its glamour for the men who had 'seen the elephant' or been in a battle.

As a Confederate soldier wrote home to his family: 'The scene was grand but it was terrible, and when I closed my eyes about 4 o'clock the next morning, I could see regiments charging and retreating, men falling and yelling, horses and men torn and mangled and myriads of horrid spectacles.'

As the fighting moved over the countryside through the rest of the summer, the newspaper writers and artists, known as the Bohemian Brigade, travelled with the troops, reporting on the battles step by step. Many times the army and government officials blasted off in anger 'at the restless brains of the press gang' for writing about the movements of the troops. This often gave information to the other side, and endangered the lives of the men.

In September, something else was putting civilian lives in danger. In the vicinity of La Crosse, a town in western Ohio, people were being 'badly scared by the monster...'

16

DECEMBER DARKNESS

HE monster roving the countryside had 'been out of the water four times, continuing his depredation in the cornfields of Harry Munger'. The hungry monster turned out to be a rhinoceros – an escapee from Dan Rice's circus, while it was travelling to a show in Lima, Ohio.

The rhino had been trained to walk around the circus ring without any harness or lead ropes, giving the crowds a thrill to be so near such an incredible looking animal. Hopefully the renegade rhino was re-united with the circus, for there's no further report about him.

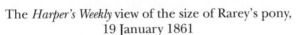

The *Harper's Weekly* view of the size of Rarey's pony,
19 January 1861

The paper did mention however, in the 18 September 1861 *Ohio State Journal*, that there was something different at the Franklin County Fair this year.

One new feature is the entry by Mr J. S. Rarey, of four full blood Shetland ponies. They were imported by Mr Rarey direct from the Shetland

133

Islands. One of these ponies is really a curiousity. We should think it is scarcely 24 inches in height, and not larger than a common sized house dog. It is five years old; and we presume, is the smallest of the horse kind in America. We understand that Mr Rarey intends breeding from this lot, and introducing them among stock-raisers. We are sorry the celebrated horse is not on exhibition, for his great reputation for eating raw grooms would have attracted to him considerable notice.

After being so long in the spotlight in such a serious way, it must have been fun to show the Shetlands: tiny hooves trotting about the ring, bushy manes and tails shaking back and forth in the sunshine; voices calling to each other when separated, high-pitched whinnies to discover how far away their friends were.

Further into the autumn, another type of pony was in the news. On 24 October, the first transcontinental telegraph message signalled an end to the Pony Express. The message relayed from Chief Justice Stephen Field in California to President Lincoln in Washington DC, stated that California was staying loyal to the Union. As one reporter put it, 'the West is all one great eagle scream'. The success of the telegraph no doubt brought a sigh of relief to the exhausted ponies and horses tired of the big rush.

People were growing weary of this six-month war which showed no signs of ending. As the papers said, 'the drum tap rattles through the land'. In late November an incident at sea flared into a blaze of international controversy – the Trent Affair. The British Mail Packet, the Trent, was intercepted by a Northern war ship. Two Southern men, James Mason and John Slidell, were taken as prisoners to Boston. This infuriated the South, and Europe was outraged at this breach of the neutrality of the sea.

Demands were raised in England to wage war with the Northern states, but Queen Victoria stated she did not desire another war. She would not shrink from conflict, but the horrible carnage of the recent Crimean War was close to her heart. In the midst of this public uproar, the Queen was struggling with a grave personal crisis.

Prince Albert had fallen seriously ill with high fevers, sleeplessness, pains and chills. He was only forty-two years old, but was exhausted from continual overwork, and depressed by the loss of two close friends to typhoid fever. These friends were also his first cousins, King Pedro of Portugal and the King's brother.

Informed of the raging Trent controversy, Prince Albert dragged himself from bed and worked out a solution, by modifying the demands of Parliament. Sending off the document, he returned to bed and sank yet deeper. By the second week of December, he was slipping in and out of consciousness. On the morning of Saturday 14 December, the hope for his recovery was fading.

Throughout the afternoon, his children came to say their final farewells. In Berlin, Princess Victoria was overwrought with anxiety that she could not come to 'her dearest papa's' bedside. In the dark of that December evening, Prince Albert's breathing became laboured. The Queen rushed to his side and watched with terror as Prince Albert, clasping her hand, quietly breathed his last.

In despair, the Queen dropped to her knees and the depths of darkness closed about her. Stunned, she was helped to the Red Room and there dissolved into a private expression of her grief. Shortly after, she gathered her children about her and they shared their desolation. The doctor, Sir James Clark, and Lord Alfred Paget came in to comfort her. Lord Paget tearfully assured her that 'he had been in waiting at her marriage, and was in waiting now'.

Prince Albert had succumbed to typhoid fever, yet recent medical guesswork suggests he may have also suffered from cancer of the stomach. The British nation had lost an honest man, a brilliant man, and Her Majesty had lost her Prince. Her world instantly turned as black as the clothes she wore forever after.

As the awful news reached America, and Ohio, Rarey must have felt a personal grief for this man who had helped him, like so many others, at the outset of his career.

A general wave of sympathy flowed across the ocean to Queen Victoria, and her position was seen in a new light. As Thurlow Weed, an influential journalist and political leader, later wrote to the *New York Times* on 26 January 1862:

> if our people knew how good and true a friend to America the Queen is, they would feel that we are not likely to be wronged in her day. Her Majesty is in deep affliction now – in Prince Albert she had both a devoted husband and a discreet counsellor. But though fully realizing the magnitude of her bereavement, she bears up under it with Queenly fortitude.

The sting of the Trent Affair was overshadowed by the tragedy. The American Secretary of State, William Seward, accepted Prince Albert's compromise; Mason and Slidell were set free, and the crisis was over.

Rarey went on in the latter days of this December to the windy city – Chicago, Illinois. Chicago, which had railings along the streets for people to hold on to when the wind blew, perhaps reminded him and his ponies of those breezy Shetland Islands. He had come to Chicago to give lectures at Bryan Hall on Saturday evening 21 December and on Christmas Eve.

Cruiser stayed at home this time, for the advertisement in *The Chicago Times* stated that 'Cruiser's muzzle and halter will be shown, and an account of his taming given.' Rarey may have felt that subjecting him to boxcars and railroads at this snowy time of year was too risky.

Appearing at another theatre in Chicago, Kingsbury Hall, on this same weekend was the diminutive General Tom Thumb, P. T. Barnum's former associate. Tom Thumb, whose real name was Charles Stratton, had brought along his little hay-burners too, for the advertisements noted that 'The General will ride in his beautiful miniature carriage (pulled by miniature horses) from the Sherman House to the Hall – previous to each entertainment.'

If Tom Thumb and Rarey ever crossed paths in Chicago, they would have certainly had a lot in common to talk about; having both been in the presence of Queen Victoria, and having seen the major capitals of Europe.

Rarey's nephew, Charles Fairrington, the twenty-four-year-old son of his sister Elizabeth, was living in Chicago. It seems likely that this is what prompted Rarey to go there in the frosty season. Since his shows were on the brink of the holidays, perhaps he had Christmas dinner and plum pudding with Fairrington and his wife.

The New Year 1862 came, and January passed, and as the ice of February crackled underfoot, Rarey was packing his passport again. At the invitation of Charles Fairrington, Rarey was preparing to travel to New York and then on to Cuba for some performances. Fairrington's wife had become ill and he was advised to take her somewhere warm, like Cuba, to regain her health.

Rarey was leaving as yet another shock of sadness gripped the country. While black shadows rested on many a home in America, this time its hand was upon the White House. In the third week of February, the Lincolns' third son, eleven-year-old Willie, was desperately ill with fevers. The President and Mrs Lincoln were beside themselves with worry and spent night after night by his bedside. Tragically, on the 20th, a Thursday afternoon, young Willie died.

Now the first families of both nations had been struck and robbed of loved ones by typhoid. Prince Alfred, the second son of Queen Victoria, had just left Havana, Cuba to sail for home after receiving the grim news about his father. In Cuba, deadly diseases were running rampant, and many children were dying from smallpox and scarlet fever. Cuba did not seem like a desirable destination at the moment, but Rarey still boarded the steamship The Columbia in New York, at Pier No. 4 on the North River. The Columbia set its compass for Havana, with Captain R. Adams of the United States Navy in command.

The *New York Times* correspondent in Cuba, who signed his dispatches LARA, sent in the following article with a dateline – Havana 1 March 1862. It was published in the Thursday 6 March edition.

> The Columbia, on her last voyage from New York, brought us, among other passengers, Mr Rarey, the celebrated horse-tamer, who it is said, proposes to give some of his extraordinary performances during his temporary sojourn here.

It was a risky sojourn, for besides the smallpox and diseases, a civil war was raging over control of the island. Food was scarce due to the conflict, and adding to the problems, the hot wet weather turned threatening. The correspondent said, 'A sudden storm of wind sprang up, and scared half the city out of their wits besides frightening the remainder.'

Havana was also reeling from a massive hunt for escaped slaves, and a raucous Masquerade Carnival. There were random killings in the streets, and a prominent businessman was murdered during the confusion of the Carnival. When authorities found the killers, they confessed that after the murder, they had planned to hijack the steamship Columbia and commandeer her back to New York.

LARA in his next column 'News from Havana' dated Saturday 15 March, published on 23 March in the *New York Times*, brought up Rarey's name again, writing:

> Now that the Carnival is over, the approaching exhibition of Mr Rarey, and his wonderful performances in taming wild horses will draw together an immense assemblage. He is advertised to give two performances, one on Saturday next (22 March) and the other on the

following day Sunday. No doubt the latter will be the best attended, for Sunday in this country is the principal day for all sorts of amusements.

The following weeks of 'News from Havana' did not include any notice of Rarey's exhibitions at Chiari's, where equestrian troupes and circuses often performed. Sara Lowe Brown, however, mentions in her book *The Horse Cruiser*, that at the first lecture in Cuba:

> His talk was interpreted to the audience, but he writes in his diary that he was 'convinced that they had no idea or appreciation of my art'. At the second exhibition, he had no interpreter. He simply illustrated his method, first by attempting to ride the horse before taming him, and second, by taming him and riding him afterward. This aroused their interest but did not enlighten them as to the method; they clung to the idea that they had witnessed a struggle like a bull-fight. 'Probably,' he says, 'they would have been better pleased had blood been spilled. I am glad there were present a number of Cubans who were anxious that some of my principles might be instilled…[into those] whose only thought was to beat the poor creatures under them and over which they were permitted to exercise the authority of master.'

While Rarey was away in Cuba, a book review appeared in the *New York Times* on 9 April 1862, for *Nolan's System for Training Cavalry* by Kenneth Garrard, Captain 5th Cavalry, New York. The book outlined 'the celebrated system of Nolan – the authority on Military Equitation in the English Army…combined with the new principles laid down by Baucher…to this treatise Capt. Garrard has added a chapter on "Rarey's Method of Taming Horses"'.

The question arises, given the countless piracies of Rarey's books, whether he knew about his method being added to this book. Rarey had won the plagiarism lawsuit in 1857, yet this did not seem to deter others from doing the same thing. After he became famous, the piracies increased tenfold. In disgust, he gave up trying to stop them, for he 'didn't have a taste for legal matters'.

The shoe had been on the other foot in the summer of 1859, when Rarey was accused by Denton Offutt of plagiarizing his book, published in 1846, *A Method of Gentling Horses, their Selection, and Curing their Diseases.* The lawsuit was dismissed. Sections of Offutt's book were arranged in a similar way to those in Rarey's work, and a few training suggestions were similar; but there was no word for word identity.

In no way though, did Offutt have the same consideration for horses as Rarey. Offutt wrote of being kind and gentling horses, but he also gave advice such as the following for runaway horses: 'You may hold any horse by fastening in the gristle of his nose a ring, and fastening the reins in it; this will hold the worst of horses.'

Offutt was a strange character, described as a 'garrulous, boastful, harum-scarum kind of man'. He tried and failed at several trades. In 1831 he decided to open a general store in New Salem, Illinois, twenty miles north of Springfield. He hired a clerk to run the store who had just taken a flatboat to New Orleans for him, a man named Abraham Lincoln.

Now running the nation, President Lincoln was shaken again on 6 and 7 April by another Union defeat at the Battle of Shiloh in Tennessee. At this 'haunting nightmare' 24,740 men became casualties of war in two days. Ironically, *shiloh* means peace in Hebrew.

On 6 May, even though the news of departures was so prevalent, the quiet death of the eloquent writer Henry David Thoreau, must have saddened many people. He was only forty-four years old when tuberculosis ended his life. After having spent his life immersed in describing the wonders of nature, his last words were simply 'Moose. Indian'.

During May, Lincoln appealed for new volunteers. Soldiers were being sacrificed in great numbers and such was Lincoln's agony that guards by his door heard him moaning in his sleep. The call was answered, for a notice appeared soon after: 'The 61st Regiment under Colonel Scheich left Columbus, Ohio for Washington DC last night. Several thousand men were collected at Columbus yesterday and hundreds are arriving by every train.'

Was Ohio's most celebrated horseman among those collected? Not yet. Rarey had volunteered earlier, but his service was being reserved for a later date. As a general rule, entertainers were considered to be valuable in uplifting the troops during the grim days. The need for a temporary escape from the pressures and intense sadness was seen in the fact that eleven large circus companies toured during the war years.

Barnum's Museum in New York was having record crowds and in May was hosting The Grand National Dog Show. Barnum's advertisements ran: 'The Bow Wow's are having their day at Barnum's and the people by the tens of thousands are enjoying the sight of them.' Dogs and horses were always a sure way to bring out a crowd; yet as May passed the mid-point, horses took over the spotlight in the city. An advert appeared in the Wednesday 21 May *New York Times*, announcing that someone with an equine mind was back in town.

> Rarey the Horse Tamer at the Cooper Institute. Arrrangements have been entered into with J. S. Rarey, who is about to return to his farm in Ohio, to give his interesting and instructive entertainments on May 27, 29, 30, and a Saturday matinee on the 31st. The only series of lectures he will be able to give in New York during the present season.

On the 26th the adverts added: 'Mr Rarey proposes to subject a perfectly unbroken colt to a continued course of tuition on the three evenings.' Then, as in Washington DC, Rarey was changing the building to suit his shows, for the advert continued:

> We understand that in consequence of the alterations made at Mr Rarey's wish in the stage of the large hall, it will be the best location for a soiree of horses and their tamer to be found in the city. An immense gathering of male and female fashionable equestrians may be confidently anticipated.

The exhibition hall at the Cooper Institute could hold 3,000 people in the cushioned iron chairs. When it first opened in November 1857, as Rarey was sailing for England, the *New York Times* described the hall as 'a huge chamber which extends under the sidewalk. By means of glass, it will receive a supply of light from heaven during the day. In night time, gas blazing forth from numerous chandeliers will supply the place of sunshine.'

Earlier in the month of May 1862, the Cooper Institute had hosted Dr Colton with his demonstration of the effects of laughing gas. It was to be hoped that the residue was not going to make the horses giddy. Something no one usually laughs about is ticket prices. The tickets for Rarey's shows were now listed at 50 cents, reserved seats 25 cents extra. A few two-dollar seats on the platform were also available.

The lectures were entitled 'The Horse – its Nature, Habits and Teaching, according to Rarey's Experience, Combined with the Science of Breaking In and Training the Wildest and Most Vicious Horses'. Another new twist this year was presenting 'the thorough education for the saddle in an incredibly short space of time'. Rarey was either tired of saying the same thing over and over, or else he knew that people would want to see something new.

On 27 May as the rain poured down, Rarey began his first lecture at the Institute. The *New York Times* on 29 May told of a dangerous accident at the beginning of the show:

> Mr Rarey experimented on three horses, one of which was a vicious brute, that just before being brought upon the stage, kicked the groom in attendance, and completely demolished a glass door. The poor fellow was much hurt, and conveyed to his house on a litter. Of course when Mr Rarey took the animal it was soon subdued, at least comparatively speaking soon, but not without a severe struggle.

At his lecture on the 29th, while he was working with a young chestnut colt, he brought up the point that 'the most important lesson to teach the horse is that of standing still', and, the *New York Times* noted, 'encouraged his maternal hearers by assuring them that colts are more easily governed than children'. He knew what he was talking about!

The advertisements for his next exhibition proclaimed:

> His last appearance and only Conversational Matinee, previous to his quitting New York. Commences at 3 o'clock Saturday afternoon. Upon this occasion, Mr Rarey wants to inform the public that he will be happy to reply to All Questions which may be addressed to him by any Lady or Gentleman, respecting his mode of managing and taming the horse. A special opportunity is offered to ladies on this occasion to send in horses possessing any vice, and to be instructed in their proper management.

It would be interesting to know the questions posed and answers given, but no written accounts were published thereafter. Over the next few days while Rarey was on the road to Ohio, all the talk in the papers was war news. That the war did not sweep into oblivion only men of age and their horses was told in the account given in the *New York Times* on 5 June:

> A fifer and drummer were found close together. The fifer sitting leaning against a tree – a ball in his heart, his fife clasped in his fingers. The Drummer boy seems to have been his companion and was in the act of supporting the expiring fifer in his arms when he himself was killed by a ball going through his head. His drum lay at his feet.

The war, all wars. What a price.

17

BLUEPRINTS AND BATTLE PLANS

$\mathcal{I}$N THE summer of 1862, Cruiser looked vibrant, his eyes lively, his step light, and his coat shining like glossy dark velvet. The Ohio sun was bright and hot, and the grass grew all around. The other Ohio son, John Rarey, was very glad to see Cruiser again, to stroke his face and watch him running in the paddock.

Back at last from his journeys, Rarey was wondering what to do next. He needed a rest from the trials of touring, so he decided he'd further his long-held goal of a new book on horses. Upstairs in his study in the cool of the morning, he sat and thought and worked out an outline of how he envisioned the book.

He decided to divide the book into four parts. The first section would cover the role of horses in ancient history, art and poetry; second – the various breeds of horses throughout the world; third – training and breeding; fourth – an overview of performing horses in circuses and shows, past and present.

He also worked on a plan for establishing an American Horse Association, a national organization with meetings held yearly in varying locations. Prizes would be given for the top horses of their breeds. Literary efforts would also be encouraged by having awards for the best equine essays. One of the essay prizes was to be 'The Rarey Medal' sponsored by an investment he'd made in government bonds.

When the outline was finished, he made an agreement with a writer named Pliny Miles to do the research and writing of the manuscript. Miles travelled to New York to begin work in the libraries there, then went on to Europe for further research.

Rarey had never felt confident of his abilities in the art of writing. Henry Hall Dixon once mentioned this in *Sporting Magazine* saying: 'he hardly ever wrote to anyone. At the best of times he was a bad correspondent, as he felt his deficiencies of education when he put his hand to paper.'

In 1862, besides working on blueprints for a new book, Rarey was also in the midst of another kind of construction. Plans were underway to build a larger house for his mother and himself, with guest rooms to accommodate the frequent visitors. The house would be on the same site as his family's homestead, incorporating some of the original brick walls of the house his father, Adam Rarey, had built in 1826, the year before John was born.

Man grooming horse

By September, he was back teaching again, but this time for free. The *Ohio State Journal* on 2 September 1862, commented that Rarey:

> who is a sound patriot, at the suggestion of certain estimable ladies who are steadily toiling for the good of our soldiers, voluntarily tendered his services for an evening's exhibition as a benefit for the funds of the Soldier's Aid Society. His offer was gladly accepted and a splendid benefit it was. The Atheneum was literally packed with one of the most intelligent and genteel audiences that ever assembled in our city... [Columbus]
>
> After taming one horse, and exhibiting three Shetland ponies, one, a colt 20 inches high and weighing 21 pounds, was brought forward in the arms of a boy. It looked more like a shaggy dog than anything of the genus equinus – though it afterwards cantered about the stage with much activity and grace.

Next came the spirited but spoiled and vicious brute with which Mr Rarey was to try conclusions…His hind feet were aimed at the performer's personnel. These exhibitions of the brute's tender mercies towards Mr Rarey were rapidly repeated, exciting the audience as with a touch of tragic. But the calm and steady manner of Mr Rarey, as he watched the equine performance of the Highland Fling, speedily dispelled all apprehensions for his safety. His complete success with this animal elicited great applause.

The magic touch, the showmanship, the horsemanship, were still as strong as ever, but the stress was starting to surface again. He could not shake off the feeling of exhaustion that had plagued him from time to time in Europe.

As one writer observed in a chapter on Rarey in the book, *Our First Century 1776–1876*:

While thus sparing the horse, Mr Rarey evidently took an immensity of work out of himself, seemingly undergoing a sustained mental strain, in order that the horse, whose instinct is so sharp, might not see the slightest faltering in his proceedings…If, therefore, at the most critical moment, he required a riding whip or a pocket handkerchief, he called for it as coolly as one would for a glass of lemonade, or as Nelson called for the sealing wax during the bombardment of Copenhagen…He went through his work in a way that showed it to be, to him, a labor of love.

As with all stresses though, sooner or later something gives, and for Rarey, health was faltering. The unrelenting tension of the war was bringing people to the breaking point. Each battle brought more terrible losses. Many believed that if it didn't end soon, 'either the South would be crushed or the North ruined'.

By November, President Lincoln was totally frustrated by the 'overcautiousness' of General George McClellan, and replaced him with the six-foot tall General Ambrose Burnside. Now at the helm, the main thrust of Burnside's campaign plan was to reach and destroy Richmond, Virginia, the Confederate capital.

Burnside decided to engage the Confederate troops at Fredericksburg, Virginia, a town on the Rappahannock River, roughly midway between Richmond and Washington DC. He believed that his troops could cut off the road to Richmond, leaving their capital defenceless.

The editorial writers for the *New York Times* expressed grave doubts about this reasoning, for on 6 December 1862 their sentiments were: 'Burnside on the Rappahannock is in great danger of being fooled by the strategy of the Rebels…If their Army would attack there, they would either be defeated or demoralized or disabled by a great battle.'

There were many players on this deadly chess board, and the best plans were often foiled by a clever counter move. The weather threw yet another spanner in the works. It was now December, and nothing would stop the winter from coming with its raw shivering days, swollen streams, and the impossible mud of the roads.

An anonymous field correspondent for the *New York Times* noted:

It is easy to play war on paper around a blazing hearth but consider the state of affairs as they exist: instead of a substantial roof for shelter, a little contemptible strip of canvas is the soldier's apology for a kennel. The nearest approach to luxury is a meal of salt pork and adamantine biscuits, forced down the palate by the aid of rancid coffee without a particle of milk…Men upon the frosty ground with but a single blanket, weak, exhausted, sick from exposure, yet clamorously urged by the impatient populace to advance on Richmond.

Cavalry (*Harper's Weekly* May 1862, drawing by Alfred R. Waud)

And it was not only the soldiers who suffered the deprivation of army life. A letter from the Centre Grand Division, Army of the Potomac, dated Saturday 6 December said:

> Several thousand horses and mules have recently been distributed among the various divisions to supply the deficiency occasioned by hard marches and bad weather. Since the commencement of winter, the animals have suffered severely from the wet and cold. A large majority of them are without any shelter, not even having the covering of a blanket. Much difficulty has been experienced of late in getting a sufficient quantity of hay on account of the limited means of transportation by rail, and the excessively bad condition of the wagon roads.

This influx of thousands of new horses may have been the reason Rarey received the following letter:

HEADQUARTERS OF THE ARMY
WASHINGTON DC
December 6, 1862

Mr John S. Rarey,

    SIR: You are hereby authorized to visit the Army of the Potomac for the purpose of inspecting the horses and mules of the cavalry, artillery, and teams belonging to that Army. All officers of the Army of the Potomac are directed to afford every facility to Mr Rarey to make this inspection.

    By order of Major-General Halleck, General-in-Chief.

Very Respectfully,
J.C. Kelton, A.D.G.

Upon receiving the letter, Rarey packed a bag and boarded a train for Virginia. When he arrived in Fredericksburg a few days later, he saw that the armies were camped on either side of the Rappahannock River, nervously eyeing one another like two tom cats bristling for a fight.

The thick smoke of campfires circled above the trees, mingling with the sounds of rumbling wagons, and the low hum of thousands of men talking. They were talking about the past, the faraway future, anything to push away the homesickness, the pain of injuries, the fear of what the next few days would bring.

Rarey was greeted by officers who introduced him to the cavalry heads. They showed him the picket lines – the endless lines of horses in every condition, shape and form. The cavalrymen outlined the major problems they were having – the runaways, biters and kickers. Rarey gave a few demonstrations to show how his system worked, but there wasn't much time – the battle lines were being drawn.

He did have a chance however to meet 'Professor' Thaddeus Lowe, the aeronaut or balloon pilot, doing intelligence work for the Union. Up in his balloon, Lowe observed the Confederate troops and telegraphed his reports. It was hazardous work, for the balloons were a very big target, and it didn't require a direct hit to destroy one. A fragment from an exploding shell one hundred feet away could cause a fatal plummet.

Over Fredericksburg, Lowe telegraphed seeing 'grey-backs' at Skinker's Neck, five miles up the road. General Burnside, after hearing the report, ordered the pontoon bridges to be put in place to cross the river. On Wednesday night 10 December, the Union men plunged into the cold water, waist deep, to put in the bridge. But at 5 am Thursday morning, as the men desperately strove to finish, gunfire rang out and killed some of the men working.

Artillery fire was opened on Fredericksburg to silence the sharpshooters. It worked for a while but later the bullets pierced the air again. At 10 am, Burnside commanded the artillery to 'concentrate the fire of all your guns on the city and batter it down!'

Through the fog and mist, the deadly missiles flew into Fredericksburg, which had been evacuated weeks before. A *New York Times* correspondent on the scene reported: 'The shot and shell went crashing through the houses, in many cases setting them on fire, causing a dense smoke which together with the explosion of so large a quantity of powder, almost hid the city from view.'

On Friday 12 December, the bridges were finally completed. The troops surged into Fredericksburg and shamelessly ransacked the crumbling, smoking town. The Confederate soldiers who were captured 'were wretchedly clad, mostly without blankets or overcoats, but generally stout and healthy'.

Now in possession of the city, Burnside planned to attack the Confederate troops encamped behind the city limits. On Saturday morning the 13th, the Union troops began crossing the river, the dense fog and mist swallowing them up as they marched to meet their fate.

The plan was to storm the hills of Marye's Heights, but something was dreadfully wrong. The tragedy of war was unfolding once again.

18

DODGING BULLETS IN THE CIVIL WAR

'THE troops advanced to the works at ten minutes before 12 noon', the *New York Times* reported, 'at a brisk run, the enemy's guns opening on them from behind stone walls and houses, with a very rapid, terrible fire…'

The fighting at Marye's Heights was furious, desperate, insane. The Union was clearly at a disadvantage, but Burnside kept sending up line after line of soldiers to replace the fallen on the front. Six times he sent them, and they just fell and fell. General Burnside, watching the fight from the garden of the Lacy House, paced to and fro in anxious anguish.

Another person was watching the battle from a more peculiar viewpoint.

'On Saturday December 13th, 1862, the third day of the battle', Rarey wrote in his journal, 'I stood on the bluff of the Rappahannock, this side of Fredericksburg, and witnessed the battle for some time. Two or three shells fell near me. In the afternoon of the same day, through the kindness of Professor Lowe, I went up alone in a balloon to watch the fight. A shell was fired directly at me, but passed under the balloon. Had to change my location.'

For Rarey, being in that nightmare zone was indescribable. Men he had just talked to, horses he had just patted hours before, now lay dead, stiff or begging for help or a merciful release. Many soldiers said that the most bloodcurdling sound in battle was the 'agonized shriek of a wounded horse'. It was wrenching to see the desperate look in their eyes, the pitiful switching of their

Over Fredericksburg in Lowe's balloon, 13 December 1862
(Illustration by James Souder)

tails – and to be powerless to ease their suffering except for the terminal solution of a bullet. As author William Holt said in *Ride a White Horse*, 'horses would never go to battlefields if not driven there by men'.

The end for a friend on the battlefield
(*Harper's Weekly* 3 August 1861)

Attempts were made to carry the dead from the fields, but fire was opened on them. So 'our troops sleep tonight where they fought today'. By nightfall, the casualty toll was staggering: 12,653 Union men and 5,309 men in grey.

On Sunday, scattered shots rang out but there was nothing amounting to a battle. The Confederate General Robert E. Lee asked for a truce to bury the dead and it was agreed upon.

Burnside, in his headquarters, vowed to renew the fight on the morrow, but the other officers were adamant against it. Burnside had to renege. There was no way his troops 'huddled in a shattered and broken condition' could mount another attack. The decision was made to evacuate Fredericksburg.

When the news of the battle reached Ohio on Sunday, Rarey's family must have worried about whether he was among those who had been wounded or lost.

In *The History of Columbus, Ohio*, author Jacob Studer related:
On the way to church in the morning of 14 December, the people were startled by running newsboys crying 'Journal Extra – the bloodiest battle of the war. Fredericksburg in flames.' Excited groups of people gathered on corners and at public houses discussing events. Newspaper men and telegraph operators were hailed with 'Anything more from the Rappahannock?' By evening, the office was crowded with people nervous for news.

A storm was raging in Fredericksburg on Monday night, the moaning wind driving a heavy downpour of rain. In the dark, the bedraggled troops left behind the crumbling ruins of Fredericksburg, and so many of their friends buried in her backyards and fields.

'Today, we behold our great army', wrote the *New York Times* on 17 December, 'its banners drooping and dripping with blood, encamped on the spot from which less than a brief week ago, it started out on its work of conquest.'

Burnside, all along doubtful of his ability to command the army, tendered his resignation, which was at first rejected, but in January General Burnside stepped down. A major shift in the war occurred on 12.01 am New Year's Day 1863, when President Lincoln signed the Emancipation Proclamation, liberating the slaves from bondage. Pen in hand he sighed, 'At last we have gotten our harpoon into the monster.'

The armies were in winter quarters now, and at last the nation's attention could be focused on lighter things. In February, the headlines stated, 'The War of Giants is pushed off the page by a Wedding of Midgets.' New York was aglow with the news that the twenty-five-year-old entertainer Tom Thumb was going to marry Lavinia Warren. Lavinia, twenty-one years old, was a warm intelligent lady of petite height: thirty-two inches and weighing twenty-nine pounds.

They had met at Barnum's American Museum, where she had been appearing. Barnum was in high glee, for their wedding promised to be the social event of the year, and it was. On Tuesday 10 February, police were called in for crowd control as the cheerful couple exchanged their vows at Grace Church in New York City. Over 2,000 guests attended the grand reception at the Metropolitan Hotel, sharing the eighty-pound wedding cake. They received gifts and congratulations from well-wishers throughout the world, including Queen Victoria.

The household of the Queen was also in a matrimonial mood, for preparations were being made for the upcoming wedding of the Prince of Wales, Edward Albert, to Princess Alexandra of Denmark. The were married on 10 March in the Chapel Royal, St George's at Windsor; the first royal wedding held there since that of Henry I in 1122. The Queen did not take part in the activities, but Princess Victoria came from Berlin, bringing her two-year-old son, Wilhelm. He created a bit of havoc during the carriage ride to Windsor by tossing his aunt's muff out of the window.

The wedding of the Prince of Wales and Princess Alexandra, March 1863
(*Illustrated London News* 1863)

When the spring blossoms of 1863 sprang forth, Rarey was home in Ohio. He kept busy with spring planting and also the excitement of foaling time; the Shetland foals were especially endearing. Rarey could enjoy watching the foals in the pasture from his window, for the ponies' paddocks and barns were across the road. The construction on his house was probably finished at this time. Cruiser had a stable and paddock built especially for him behind the house. While the construction was going on, did Cruiser keep an eye on the people working, shaking his head and flattening his ears if anyone came close? He was always up to a good game of stallion's bluff – to see who would back down first, and he enjoyed getting in a quick nip if he could.

Rarey's inclination to harmonize and work with a horse rather than against it was a major part of his personality; and perhaps the natural order for someone born in the time of Sagittarius, with its symbol of half man, half horse. It was also the key to his success. This theme surfaced in the phrenological reading he had done in New York. Phrenology was a popular science at the time, which

Cruiser in his paddock, sketched from life
(Courtesy of Mrs Elsie Rarey, Thornville, Ohio)

involved 'reading' the shape and size of the nooks and crannies of the head. As one poem went:

> Know well thy skull and note its hilly lumps;
> the proper study of mankind is bumps.

Rarey's reading, published in the *American Phrenological Journal* in March 1861, revealed the results of their exploration.

> His ability in managing animals arises from mental harmony and self possession…He has a remarkably magnetic eye – and has the power of impressing, by look and by touch, this calm sovereignty of his will. He has very large Order and does everything by method, even the subjugation and training of his own disposition and motives…He is smooth built, easy in motion, as if every joint were lubricated, and every part of his system hung on centers so as to move easily…
>
> He has great natural kindness, a full share of respect and veneration, and a love of the right and true…His feelings are quick and his intellect rapid in action, though he is not betrayed into impatience…He has an excellent power to judge of character and motive, estimates strangers at a glance, and is rarely mistaken in this first impression. This faculty enables him also to understand animals and thus comprehend their strong and weak points. For years we have observed that those in whom the Organ of Human Nature is strongly developed, have skill and capacity to train dogs, horses and oxen; to produce obedience without cruelty…

We all make mistakes, however, and Rarey's first impression of the writer Pliny Miles must have been off the mark. Miles had written to him on 20 December 1862 that the manuscript was almost ready, but Rarey never received it. What happened to Miles and the manuscript was not recorded, and remains a mystery. Rarey's hopes for his new book were dashed.

Also in a heap on the ground were his plans for another tour of England and the Continent. He felt it would be disloyal to leave America during her critical hour; and in Europe, many people had divided loyalties as to which side they supported.

Emperor Napoleon offered an elegant statement of this fence sitting nonchalance, saying; 'If the North is victorious, I shall be happy. If the South is victorious, I shall be enchanted.'

Yet as the supply of American cotton and other necessities shrank, the gravity of the situation grew more intense. By the second year of the war the *New York Times* was reporting that: 'The French Emperor is offering to join England and Russia in soliciting an armistice between the Government of the US and the rebels who are seeking its overthrow.'

Napoleon was soon dealing with attempts at his own overthrow. A plot was discovered and dissolved, involving 120 people to 'assail Napoleon with bombs, one after another until he should surely be slain', as he rode along a new boulevard.

All over the world, a spirit of revolt seemed to be rising, as people everywhere were experiencing the 'drive and push and rush and struggle of the raging, tearing, booming 19th century', as Mark Twain wrote, with his finger on the pulse of the times.

As the raging struggle of the war continued in the spring of 1863, the terrible lessons of Fredericksburg seemed to have been forgotten. At Chancellorsville, Virginia, another battle was fought during the days between 30 April to 5 May, in which there were casualties numbering 13,156 Southern men and 16,845 Union men.

Professor Lowe was there, up in his balloon, telegraphing his observations. Yet at the end of the battle, Lowe was so thoroughly sickened and disgusted by the sights he'd seen and the waste of lives, that he resigned his volunteer services for the US Signal Corps. In the face of all the carnage, growing numbers of men were again 'taking the grand bounce'. They were taking their destinies back into their own hands, even though General Halleck had announced that 'desertion from the Army is not permissable'.

President Lincoln ordered the Conscription Act, to draft every man aged between eighteen and forty-five. Later, violent protests broke out in New York City, and people were killed in the riots.

Something else was also dwindling besides volunteers for the Army – the supply of army horses. On 13 May, the War Department issued an Executive Order 'prohibiting the exportation of horses, mules, and livestock'. In the first two years of the war, 284,000 horses had been inducted into the army.

Family and farm horses were bought and thrown together with the wild horses that were dragged off the plains and shipped in from the West. It was very frightening and bewildering for all of them. No wonder contagious diseases spread like wildfire through them. Veterinary care was scarce and often futile, for the diseases progressed rapidly under the stress of camp life and the marches.

Between 1862 and 63, 100,000 horses and mules perished from a virus plague.

The historically shady business of horse trading fell to its lowest point when the word was out that the government was buying horses. Corruption was the rule, not the exception. The brutal facts were told in a report to Congress by Representative Dawes, on 13 January 1862.

> A regiment of cavalry horses has just reached Louisville [in Kentucky– a holding center for army horses] 1,000 strong, and a board of army officers has condemned 485 of the 1,000 horses as utterly worthless. The man who examined those horses declared upon his inspection that there is not one of them worth twenty dollars. They are blind, spavined, with the heaves, with glanders, and with every disease that horses are heir to...
>
> They have been sent here [Washington DC] and they have been sent there to spend the winter; and many of the horses never sent back have been abandoned – tied to posts and to trees within Washington and were left to starve to death. A guide can take you around today to the hundreds of carcasses of horses chained to trees where they have pined away, chewing on bark and limbs till they starve and die...

How people could have left those horses to starve is hard to comprehend. In the midst of all this confusion and cruelty, the Union finally established a Cavalry Bureau in July of 1863, to organize the buying, training and caring for army horses. Plans were put in motion for building a gigantic cavalry depot to hold some 12,000 horses, at Giesboro Point, Maryland, near Washington DC.

The War Department records stated that they planned a total of six depots, to help some of the wounded and sick horses 'become fit for service again, and to minimize future losses of horses such as those sustained after the Battle of Gettysburg'.

At Gettysburg, Pennsylvania, during the stifling hot days of 1, 2 and 3 July the Union clashed with the Confederate armies. This battle halted the South from bringing the battle north, but at the cost of 20,451 Confederate men, 23,045 men in blue, and some 15,000 horses.

In mid July, the North was threatened again when General John Hunt Morgan and his Confederate cavalry troops came galloping into Ohio. Burning bridges, tearing up railroad tracks, capturing horses; they spread a blaze of terror before them. They were finally caught and forced to surrender on 26 July, near Salineville, Ohio. This was north of Columbus, almost parallel with Pittsburgh, Pennsylvania. Morgan was imprisoned in Columbus, Ohio, but in November he tunnelled out and escaped. During Morgan's terrifying raids, Rarey and his family tasted the anxiety of the war coming to their doorstep, something the people in the South had to deal with continually.

In 1863, Rarey was called again to serve the Union as a buyer of horses and as a cavalry inspector. One profile stated that he made his inspections 'with considerable discretion'.

The trail of his life disappears into blanks here. There are few references to his activities in the years of 1863, 1864, and early 1865; excepting that his health still troubled him and he was living quietly in Groveport, and acquired some unusual animals.

19

A RING AROUND THE CIRCUS

'*M*r Rarey trained a team of elks', wrote George Bareis in *The History of Madison Township* (Franklin County, Ohio), 'which he frequently drove in the neighborhood and to Columbus.'

In the red leather journal in which Rarey had written about the Edinburgh kicking mare, there was a notation in the back page by a relative that she 'remembered Rarey coming to church with two reindeer attached to a sleigh'.

Whether they were elks or reindeer, he must have had a very good time driving them about, smiling at the looks on people's faces. Rarey had a love of the unusual and a flair for the dramatic; as when he had the London Zoo ship their furious zebra over to him.

The circus man Dan Rice also trained an odd assortment of animals, including a giraffe, buffalo, rhino (the Ohio water monster) and an educated pig named Lord Byron who would answer questions with various grunts.

In the early months of 1865, Rarey began to hear the music of the circus again. The war was dragging on, but the South's supplies and army were severely depleted, though their spirit was not and they stood to their cause. The Union was cautiously optimistic, however, that the war was coming to a close.

Encouraged by the news, Rarey made arrangements to tour with Cruiser in the Northeastern states with Silas O. Wheeler's Great International Circus. Rarey and Cruiser were to be featured as the opening attraction, for the first hour of the show. So in April, they

158

heard the wail of the steam engine whistle in their ears again, while riding the rails to the East.

Wheeler's Circus opened its travelling season on 26 April in the Pavilion at the Boston City Fair Grounds, in Massachusetts. The advertisements in various newspapers proclaimed:

> The Indomitable Rarey engaged. The Proprietor has great pleasure in announcing that he has, at an immense cost, effected an arrangement with J. S. Rarey, the World-Renowned Horse-Tamer! who will give a series of public exhibitions and lectures; practical and demonstrative of his system…It is Rarey's system to teach the horse instead of breaking him…In illustrating his theory, Mr Rarey will introduce Lord Dorchester's universally famous English horse Cruiser! Upon whom he first displayed in England the might and magic of his art…The veritable Cruiser, although getting old [13 years old] is still a fine specimen of an English thoroughbred. Mr Rarey will deliver his lecture and exhibit Cruiser, afternoon and evening…He invites everyone having vicious or hitherto unmanageable horses, no matter what their temper or how badly broken they may have been, to bring them to the Circus on the day of the exhibition, either in the afternoon or evening. He will not only subdue the most savage and furious of them by kind and gentle means, but also in his hour long lectures, instruct their owners how to do it themselves…Doors open at 2 and 7 o'clock.

S. O. WHEELER'S
Great International
CIRCUS !
Organized for the Travelling Season of 1865.

STUPENDOUS ATTRACTION !

RAREY,
The Indomitable Rarey, engaged.   Besides a
full and brilliant
EQUESTRIAN TROUPE,
Comprising most of the conspicuous Riders,
Gymnastic Artists and Clowns in
the Profession.

Circus advertisement (*Danbury Evening News* 1 June 1865)

Among the 'galaxy of talent' in this circus troupe, Rarey had an assortment of horsemen and women to chat with, for the ads listed: Eaton Stone, a bareback rider and Wild Horseman of the Pampas; Charles Sherwood, a juvenile master performing Olympic Feats on Horseback; J. H. Roff an Equestro-Comedian; and Mrs Stone, the Model Equestrienne. Other acts included: Jeanette Ellsler, the daring Tight Rope Artiste; Nat Austrix, the Comic Australian Genius and Laughing Philosopher; and John Foster, the Shakespearean Jester.

Initially, Rarey was only scheduled for the four dates in Boston, but he remained with the circus after that. The excitement of the shows, the clapping of the audience perhaps ignited the old flame of performing for him again. The travelling agenda was a gruelling one, however, with shows practically every day in towns throughout Massachusetts.

By the middle of May, they were in Rhode Island. The treasurer for Wheeler's Circus was Augustine Conant. In an interview for the *Providence Sunday Journal* on 14 April 1912, Conant recalled the two-day stand and street parade there in 1865.

'…ours was sort of a triumphal march. We had a little band wagon and a few vehicles in which we carted our tent and other articles of a circus outfit. There were no animals in that parade, that is of a wild beast order; neither were there any glittering uniforms. We were just a plain, everyday circus.'

While the parade was parading, the canvas men and twelve assistants put the tents and seats up. By two o'clock in the afternoon, it was show time. After Rarey's lecture, the performers made their entrance. Conant remembered;

'We always had an eight and a twelve horse entry for the quadrilles and then came the usual pad-saddle riding, the horizontal bars, the trapeze act, some somersault business, a contortion act and then the special feature always reserved for the last – the bareback riding.'

After Rhode Island, the circus played dates throughout Connecticut, averaging some twenty miles a night between towns. The canvas men took the tents down as soon as the last spectators left, around 11 pm, then the wagons would be packed and ready to go. The troupe would have a meal at the hotel, and then it was off into the night.

The circus caravans would sometimes get lost on the dark roads.

They also suffered other calamities such as falling in ditches and breaking the wagon wheels, and encountering small bridges which collapsed under the weight of the wagons. Another obstacle was the opposition in many towns by the local clergy to circus entertainment. Managers often softened the clergy's viewpoint and those of the town's selectmen with free passes to the show.

When Wheeler's Circus was in Bridgeport, Connecticut, the *Bridgeport Evening Standard* on Wednesday 31 May mentioned that: 'Very many persons have expressed surprise and regret that our authorities should have licensed a show to perform here on Fast Day evening...our best citizens would be highly gratified if the license could even now be revoked.'

The writer, however, must have pushed aside his indignation, and went off to the show, for in the Friday 2 June edition of the paper: 'The circus in the evening sent out their band and the tent was crowded. If anything could excuse such a performance on such a day, it was the exhibitions of Mr John S. Rarey in horse taming which were certainly astonishing...'

On Saturday 3 June, the paper reported:

On Thursday afternoon, Mr Rarey took for his subject upon which to operate, a dark chestnut horse belonging to P. F. Barnum Esq. of this city. The horse was a biting and kicking beast which could not be controlled. Mr Rarey, after a few minutes manipulation quieted him and rendered him as docile and harmless as a kitten. Mr B informs us today he has been in the stable with and handled him with impunity, and that he is as gentle as a lamb. His entire nature seems to be changed.

The owner of the dark chestnut horse was most probably P. T. Barnum, for his home base was Bridgeport, Connecticut, where he was one time even the mayor. The article also refers to him as Mr B in the second half.

Wheeler's Circus held shows in the Connecticut towns of Norwalk, Danbury, and on 5 June in Waterbury. After the show in Waterbury, the association between Rarey and Silas Wheeler was severed. The *New York Sunday Mercury* on 11 June, reported that: 'Rarey, we hear, has retired from Wheeler's International Circus, and intends giving exhibitions on his own hook. He is to be at Hartford [Connecticut] on the 12th.'

Rarey may have grown tired of the stress and bustle of two shows a day, or what is usually behind such breaks – money. It seems that

Rarey was back in Ohio by July, for there was a note in a family record that on 13 July 1865, Rarey was visited at home by General William Tecumseh Sherman. General Sherman was from Lancaster, Ohio, which is southeast of Columbus.

The war had finally ended on 9 April, when both sides acknowledged it was 'useless to prolong the slaughter'. Riding his faithful grey horse Traveller, the Confederate General Robert E. Lee rode to the McLean House near Appomattox Court House in Virginia. There he met the Union General Ulysses S. Grant, and they came to terms to end the war. News travelled slowly and far flung troops continued fighting until 14 April, when the official end of hostilities was declared.

At Fort Sumter in South Carolina, retired Major-General Robert Anderson raised the same American flag he had taken down four years before. As the newspapers shouted the news, celebrations burst forth in the North with parades, bells ringing, and the peaceful boom of cannons.

When a man from the South came to call at the White House, Lincoln remarked during their conversation: 'I love the Southern people more than they love me. My desire is to restore the Union. I do not intend to hurt the hair of the head of a single man in the South, if it can possibly be avoided.'

In the afternoon of Friday 14 April, President and Mrs Lincoln took a ride in their carriage, talking about old times and making plans for going home to Illinois when his term was finished. During the ride he turned to her saying, 'I've never been so happy in my life.' Here at the pinnacle of his greatest hour, the ending of the war, personal disaster loomed only hours away in the night at Ford's Theatre. For at 10.22 that evening, while the Lincolns and friends Major Henry Rathbone and his fiancée Clara Harris were watching the play *Our American Cousin*, a man of evil intent was stealing up behind them.

The bitterly deranged actor John Wilkes Booth opened the door, put a gun to Lincoln's head and fired. The President slumped forward, immediately unconscious. Mrs Lincoln screamed in terror while Booth wrestled with Major Rathbone, stabbing him with a dagger. Booth then leapt off the balcony, eleven feet through the air, to the stage below, breaking his leg on contact. Shouting 'Sic Semper Tyrannis [thus always to tyrants]' he fled out of the side door.

Lincoln was still breathing as he was being carried out of the theatre to the Petersen house across the street. There he was placed in a cramped back bedroom, attended by doctors, friends and the grieving, sobbing Mrs Lincoln. At 7.22 the following morning, his life was over.

As the telegraphs gave the shocking news across the country, 2,000 soldiers were galloping out of Washington, in search of Lincoln's murderer. Crowds of people gathered together in town squares, numb with horror and disbelief. Jacob Studer in *The History of Columbus, Ohio* related that people were:

> tearfully discussing the dire calamity which in the very hour of its deliverance had befallen the country. A somber spirit invaded, as though death's shadow had fallen upon every spirit. A dispatch that Mr Lincoln had expired blotted out many hopes fondly cherished he would survive his injuries. During an eulogy given, there were heads bowing in grief, eyes wet with sorrow or flashing with indignation and abhorrence of the murderous deed which deprived the nation of its chief.

The Secretary of State, William H. Seward, had also been savagely attacked by Booth's accomplice Lewis Paine. He approached Seward as he lay on a sick bed, and then fighting off his attendants, he slashed Seward's face, cutting his cheek to the bone. Fortunately Seward survived his injuries. He slowly recovered, and continued as Secretary of State.

A $100,000 reward was put out for the capture of Lincoln's killer. A massive manhunt went on until 26 April, when Booth and his friend David Herold were finally tracked down to a tobacco barn near Port Royal, Virginia, about sixty miles from Washington. They refused to come out, so the barn was set on fire. Herold finally surrendered, but Booth had no intentions of coming out alive. He did, but he was mortally wounded while being captured. He was shot in the back of the head, almost exactly in the spot he shot Lincoln. Booth died shortly after.

Eight conspirators in the assassination plot were brought to trial. Three received life sentences and hard labour, one got a term of six years hard labour, and the four others received the sentence to be hung by the neck until dead. David Herold, Lewis Paine, George Atzerodt, and Mrs Mary Surratt were hanged before a restless crowd on 7 July 1865.

Booth and Herold desperately escaping after the dastardly deed was done (*Harper's Weekly* 1865)

The plot had ended in death for all the principal players involved. Vice-President Andrew Johnson was sworn in as the new President, as the flags fluttered at half mast, and everything was draped in black. A funeral train was prepared with a portrait of Lincoln on front, to carry him home to Illinois. In another compartment was the casket of Lincoln's son Willie, who had died in 1862, now going home with his father to rest. The train stopped in numerous towns and cities on the way, so that people could pay their respects. Many were the same towns he had visited while en route to Washington in February 1861. In Springfield, Lincoln's horse, Old Bob, now sixteen years old, was covered with a special blanket and led in the funeral procession behind the hearse.

The country had to go on and, now that the war was over, the soldiers and their horses could at last go home – the ones that remained. 618,000 soldiers had died in the war, 100,000 civilians perished, and between 1,200,000 and 1,500,000 horses and mules died while serving the men who held their reins.

As the summer of 1865 flowed on into August, Rarey picked up the threads of his career and resumed his lectures. This time he went farther up north, to Montreal, Quebec. He gave several performances there on 10, 11 and 12 August.

Eventually, he returned home, and when Groveport officials were planning a big barbecue at the Fair Grounds, they asked Rarey to help liven it up. Frank Tallmadge, in *Horseback Riding In and Around Columbus*, wrote that Rarey promised:

> an escort of 50 men and 50 women in the saddle, and he made good, with the added attraction of two youngsters on Shetlands – one dressed as General Washington and one as Lafayette. Mr Rarey on Cruiser led the escort, with these boys at his side, meeting the Columbus delegation at the Walnut Creek bridge. This occasion proved to be Cruiser's last public appearance.

As the leaves fell and the chill in the air deepened with the coming of December, John Rarey gathered with family and friends for his 38th birthday. The cold of the coming winter was already sliding icy fingers across the hills and valleys of Ohio. By 16 December, the ponds were frozen to stillness, and Rarey went ice skating with some friends on a Saturday night. The skating was fun, but unbeknown to them, the evening ahead held disaster.

20

A STROKE OF MISFORTUNE

*R*ETURNING to his house after skating, Rarey started to have a strange uncomfortable feeling. He couldn't shake it off. He could feel something was going wrong – and it did.

'We regret to learn', the *Columbus Dispatch* reported on 22 December, 'that John S. Rarey Esq. of Groveport, was attacked in the left side with paralysis, last Saturday evening. He had returned but a little while before from a skating frolic and was entertaining some friends when, feeling faint, he walked out towards the stables and was attacked as stated and taken into the house.'

His friends were frightened. They didn't know what had happened to him out there in the night. They only knew they had found him lying on the ground. After being helped into the house, Rarey was unable to tell them that he had been overcome with dizziness and fell, and then he couldn't move. He had suffered a stroke. In the jumble of days that followed, the paralysis of his left arm and leg seemed like an insurmountable wall. He had never felt so horrible and so frightened in all his life.

Yet all was not taken away; so many people helped and cared, and the stroke had not stolen his power of speaking or writing. Twelve days later, he was writing a letter to the newspaper:

Editor,   Groveport
Ohio State Journal   December 28th 1865

The kind notice, in your paper of the 18th, of my terrible affliction having caused considerable anxiety in the minds of many friends far

166

and near, will you please state for me through the columns of your widely circulated and valuable paper for the satisfaction of those whom it may concern, that through the Providence of God and the kind and skillful attentions of Dr W. L. Lehaney and Dr S. M. Smith of Columbus, I am slowly recovering and expect soon to be among my friends again.

Jno. S. Rarey

Letter from John Rarey to the *Ohio State Journal* (Reproduced by permission of the Ohio Historical Society)

As always, his friends included those with manes and tails. He knew that for him, the best medicine was horses. Frank Tallmadge related that when Rarey was sick 'his ponies were brought to the unfurnished back parlour of his home'. He probably asked for Cruiser too, to be brought over to the back door to visit him.

Strokes can destroy the sections of the brain which control movement. Often, however, the brain can gradually make new connections around the site of injury. The person can then regain some or all of the use and control of the parts of the body stricken. For Rarey, seeing Cruiser and his ponies were probably his most cheerful moments in the early weeks of recovery.

The New Year of 1866 was certainly off to a dismal start. Rarey was embarrassed by his infirmity. He didn't want to see friends, but they kept calling, looking at him with sad eyes. He longed to go where he wanted, do what he wanted, and not be so dependent on others, taking their time. He was grateful, however, to those helping, especially his niece Mrs Elizabeth Williams, the daughter of his sister Margaret. Mrs Williams was a young widow, kind at heart, who went out of her way to help him be comfortable.

By early spring, he was regaining some of his strength. He was determined to find a cure and live a normal life, and not wallow in self pity. So many men had returned from the war with far greater atrocities – missing legs, feet, arms and hands. As in the past, he put his trust in new horizons. Someone, somewhere must have a new treatment that would work; or perhaps a change in diet, climate or water would be the key. He heard that some people found relief while bathing in or drinking the waters of mineral springs. Others reported better results when it was mixed with champagne. It was worth a try.

There was a famous spa resort in White Sulphur Springs, West Virginia, where in the bubbling waters a woman had been miraculously healed long ago. In the early summer, Rarey journeyed south to White Sulphur Springs. Mrs Williams probably accompanied him. There in the beautiful misty hills, they checked in at the Grand Central Hotel, later known as the Old White [presently The Greenbrier]. In 1860, the Prince of Wales had stayed there during his American tour.

Rarey enjoyed the spacious rooms, the springhouse, and the beauty of the mountains, but no miracles happened. The road before him was open again. They returned to Ohio and the hot summer days came and went. He heard of a doctor in Cleveland, Ohio, who specialized in his condition and decided to go and see what he had to say. During August, he was making arrangements to travel to Cleveland and, being a practical man, wanted to make sure everything was taken care of while he was away. He wrote his last will and testament.

On the last day of August, his family friends, Charles Pontius (Rarey's mother's maiden name was Pontius) and Frederick Bunn (possibly his sister Margaret's son-in-law, for he had a niece – Mrs Sarah Jones Bunn) came over to be his witnesses to the signing of his will, and they agreed to be the executors of the estate.

In the beginning of September, John Rarey and Mrs Williams arrived in Cleveland, a city with miles of riding trails which were known as the 'green necklace' in and around the city. They secured rooms at the Weddell House, a five-storey 200-room luxury hotel located at Superior Avenue and Bank Street, later renamed West 6th Street. The hotel was just five blocks from the shores of Lake Erie, and four blocks from the Cleveland City Hospital. In 1861, Lincoln had given a speech from the balcony of the Weddell House, while en route to his first inauguration.

Rarey visited the specialist, who offered some hope and set up a schedule to visit him every day. One remedy which Rarey probably prescribed for himself was taking a daily ride on horseback. He didn't call any attention to himself, for a man who met him in Cleveland described him as a 'mild and retiring man'.

He did enjoy being with people again, though, for the *Cleveland Herald* on 6 October said that he 'retained to a great extent, his usual brilliant colloquial powers, and often amused and edified those by whom he was constantly surrounded, with stories of his adventures in this and foreign lands. Yet he believed the hour of death was near at hand, and frequently alluded to the fact that he had all the heart could wish for, but health.'

The effects of the stroke were a frustrating hindrance. He tired easily and walked slowly, having trouble raising his left leg. This made it hard for him to go up and down the stairs at the Weddell House; so he and Mrs Williams moved to a boarding house owned by a Mrs Sanborn at 195 St Clair Street. This was just three blocks away and around the corner.

As September turned the corner to October, everything seemed to be going well, with little bits of progress here and there. When

Thursday 4 October dawned, though, tragedy struck. At about 2 o'clock in the afternoon, Rarey had just stepped outside when suddenly he felt a severe pain in his head. The pain was so intense he immediately returned to the apartment, and told Mrs Williams what was happening. She had him lie down on a lounge chair and then called for help. The specialist was unavailable, but another doctor came. The doctor checked his vital signs but didn't think it was very serious.

John Rarey, lying quietly, was heard to say: 'If I could only get back once more to the old farm and put my arms around my dear horse's neck, I believe I should get well.' But that hope was in vain, for after about an hour, he startled everyone in the room by plainly stating: 'I am dying.' He whispered a few things to Mrs Williams that he wanted to relay to his mother and family, and then unconsciousness began to overtake him. Twenty minutes later Rarey's life burned down to the quick. His breathing stilled, his heart stopped beating, and then he was gone.

21

UNFINISHED BUSINESS

OHN Rarey's hopes and dreams for the future had vanished. The dreadful news was relayed home. His forty-nine-year old brother Frederick rushed to Cleveland and with a heavy heart brought John's body back home. The funeral was held on Sunday 7 October. And the sun shone as a large crowd of friends and family followed the hearse wagon from his house to the service held at a Methodist church in Groveport. His mother Mary Catherine, in her black veil, had to face once more the loss of one of her children.

John Rarey had wished to be buried by his father in the Groveport cemetery, alongside his three sisters and two brothers, who had not survived childhood: Catherina, one year old; twins Jesse and Anna, four months; Adam S., two years; and Sarah Ann, one year old.

A simple rounded grave stone with the upraised letters of John S. on the top marked the site of burial. Rarey's will stipulated an amount of money to purchase a family monument, and that was erected at a later date.

Charles Fairrington wrote a stirring notice to the *Columbus Gazette* published on 19 October 1866:

> Rarey is Dead! Break the sad tidings gently to his noble mother who now, with the weight of 77 winters pressing her steadily to the tomb can ill afford to lose the youngest of eleven, her child, her hope, her glory. Speak tenderly of the bereavement to those whom he was more than a brother or friend. But we are not alone in our grief. We are not the only losers by this sad event. J. S. Rarey belonged not only to us –

not alone to Ohio, not alone to America! The world claims him as one
who had benefitted the race…

As the news flashes across the tamed Pacific that Rarey is no more,
methinks I see the good tenderhearted Queen in tears at the sad
announcement. And the crowned heads who vied with each other in
courtesies to the living, bowing with grief in honor of the dead. Don
Pedro II, Emperor of Brazil, said to me, 'I respect the proud fame of
your uncle…that he conquers by the irresistible power of kindness.'

He left a large fortune and a proud name, and met his fate like a
philosopher and a Christian.

There was yet another who mourned his absence, but in silence –
an aging dark bay stallion. What would become of Cruiser?
Thinking ahead for his old friend and 'Man Friday', Rarey had
included almost a whole page of instructions in his will regarding
'the care, comfort, and keeping of my stallion Cruiser'.

He gave him to his brother Frederick, along with a bay mare and
colt, with the condition that Cruiser 'is not to be used for any other
purpose than as a stallion, nor for any purposes of exhibition by
any one, at any time or place…Cruiser is to be kept and remain on
the farm where he now is, and within the enclosure and stable now
occupied by him, or similar ones, as along as he lives.' Rarey also
decreed that Cruiser, 'must be well taken care of', and 'furnished
with suitable and sufficient food and other provisions for his
comfort'. He stated too that the stable and farm be 'kept in good
repair'.

He had quite a few other horses, which he gave to his family as
follows:

> to my niece Mrs Elizabeth Williams, my bay horse, Active, and my single
> New York buggy.
>
> …my two bay match carriage horses, Billy and Jim, and my large two
> horse carriage and harness to my sister Margaret Jones, but my mother
> Mary Catherine Rarey is, during her life, to have the right to share
> with my sister Margaret, in the use of the horses, carriage and harness.
>
> …to my brother Charles W. Rarey, my two-year-old colt, Venison,
> being a dark bay stallion.
>
> …to my nephew Henry Rarey, my sorrel colt, Hansom.
>
> …to my nephew C. W. Fairrington, my sorrel colt, Dick.
>
> …to my niece Sarah E. Jones, my bay filly, Secesh.
>
> …to my brother William H. Rarey, my yearling bay stallion colt,
> Walnut.
>
> …to my sister Margaret Jones, my bay pony, Prince.

…to my nephew James Rarey, my small pony, Gipsey, said pony is now in his possession.

It's plain to see that the continued care and well being of his horses, especially Cruiser, was of utmost concern to him. He was well aware that after he was gone, there would be plenty of people ready and eager to buy Cruiser, put him on display, and capitalize on his name. Rarey felt that Cruiser would come to harm if this happened, and so tried to ensure he would enjoy a comfortable retirement.

Within a few days, notices of Rarey's passing appeared in numerous papers around the country. The *New York Times* ran a lengthy piece on 8 October, reprinted from the *Cleveland Herald*. Yet London, the scene of his greatest triumphs, only received the news, 'melancholy slow through the mail bags of Nova Scotia', as his friend Henry Hall Dixon commented in *Sporting Magazine* in November 1866. Dixon was moved by the sad news to remember Rarey, in the Omnibus column, with a warm portrait in words.

For three seasons he held the town, and everybody was anxious to see him…day after day you saw the finest horsemen of the kingdom there [at the Round House] all declaring that they couldn't keep away, and that they had never had such a treat as seeing Rarey face to face with a savage…

There was nothing weak about him, but yet there was a quiet simple-heartedness and an unaffected air and manner, which made people who saw him declare he could not be 'the' Rarey – the fellow who is always among horses. One might have thought they expected to see him with the manners and talons of the fabled dragon…

…whether he was among horse dealers or in the midst of bishops at a Suppression of Cruelty to Animal's Society, he was always the same. There never was a more social being, and he liked to see and know everyone of note, from the highest in the land, to the lady whose husband 'spoke disrespectfully of her cork leg'…

Rarey's first great hit was with Cruiser but he had some much worse subjects than him to deal with…How he ever lived so long was a wonder, as three or four times we have seen a horse's hoof within an inch of smashing his breast-bone, and yet he measured his distance to a nicety and always just got away.

We never remember his being out of temper with a horse but once, and under no provocation did we ever hear him give way to an oath or a rough expression. In fact, no one was more completely, Nature's gentleman…

Back in Groveport, as the winter of 1866 settled in, Cruiser still meandered around the paddock, but his days were empty now. As the months stretched into years, Cruiser slipped once more into a defensive attitude against people and angrily drove them away. He pinned his ears and wrinkled his nose as if to say, 'Go away and leave me alone.' His early years of contact with people were coming to the surface again in his mind.

Rarey's mother lived in the house until she died two years later, also in October, the 25th, in 1868. The house lay empty for years until Zadock Vezey, a farmer and businessman, and his wife Lizzie, bought the property in the autumn of 1874 for $24,000. They began redecorating, but didn't move in until 1875.

Rarey's house in Groveport (Illustration by James Souder)

True to Rarey's will, Cruiser was still holding court out in his stable. He was in rather good condition for a twenty-three-year old horse, but the years of grinding grain had worn his teeth down, those 'puissant' teeth of old, to such an extent that he couldn't eat hay; so he was given special soft food.

When the summer came, Cruiser was starting to look as if time were placing a hand upon him. On a Wednesday in July, the 7th day, heavy clouds released a torrent of rain. As the raindrops drummed on the barn roof, the celebrated stallion lay down for the last time.

THE LAST OF RAREY'S HORSE.

THE FAMOUS CRUISER DIES AT THE RAREY FARM, IN OHIO, AT THE AGE OF TWENTY-TWO YEARS.

From the Columbus (Ohio) State Journal, July 10.

Probably no horse was ever more generally known than the celebrated horse Cruiser, imported from England in 1861 by John S. Rarey, whose system of horse-taming was for some time the sensation in this country and England. When Mr. Rarey went to England his system was thoroughly put to the test by contact with Cruiser, an animal that was so vicious that he was closely and continuously confined in a stable, in such a way that he could by no possibility reach anybody, either with his mouth or heels. His food was delivered to him through a sort of funnel, and he seems to have been kept solely as an extremely wicked curiosity. His splendid muscle and activity gave him the widest scope for the exercise of his incorrigibility, and he is said to have kicked so high as to strike a board floor fourteen feet above the floor on which he stood. Ordinarily, it was only the work of a few minutes for Mr. Rarey to tame a horse, but it took him three hours to subdue the terrific Cruiser. After putting Cruiser under control, Mr. Rarey purchased him and brought him to this country, and placed him on the Rarey farm, at Groveport, in this county, where he became popular among breeders. He became so gentle that the people about the Rarey farm could fondle him as they would a kitten, and his colts were noted for their kind disposition. Strangers, however, were not permitted to have much to do with him. This was to prevent teasing and the revival of the old propensities.

Cruiser died at the Rarey farm on Wednesday last, in the twenty-third year of his age. His teeth were worn so much that he could not eat hay, and provender had to be specially provided for him. As contemplated by the will of Mr. Rarey, he received the kindest care in his old age, and it was only recently that he fell into a decline. From a bill dated May 4, 1861, we take the pedigree of Cruiser, as follows:

"Cruiser is of the celebrated Venison stock of England, and was sired by Old Venison, the winner of the Derby race in 1818. Venison proved himself the stoutest horse of his day, having traveled on foot in one year, when only three years old, nine hundred miles, and run fourteen races and won twelve. Cruiser was bred by Lord Dorchester in 1852, sired by Venison by Partizan, by Walton, out of Parasal by Potatoes, son of Eclipse. Cruiser's dam was Red Rover, by Tramp, out of Syntaxma, sister to Syntax, sire of Beeswing, the dam of New Minster, the most valuable stallion now in England."

Last of Rarey's horse (Headline from the *New York Times* 10 July 1875)

AT THE GREAT PAVILION,

Corner of Harrison Avenue and Newton Street,

THIS AFTERNOON AND EVENING,

And every Afternoon and Evening during the week,

RAREY,

The World-renowned Horse-Tamer,

and his celebrated horse

CRUISER,

in connection with

WHEELER'S

INTERNATIONAL CIRCUS

One of the most complete organizations of the kind ever exhibited.

The Members of the Company in their

Equestrian Feats,

Wonderful Vaultings,

Athletic Performances,

Acrobatic Displays, &c., &c.

Each entertainment will begin with

RAREY'S LECTURE,

Practically illustrated by

TAMING VICIOUS HORSES,

before the audience, which will continue about an hour.

PRICES OF ADMISSION:

Adults 50 cents ; Children 25 cents.

ap26 · · 4t

As with his partner, local and national papers carried the sad news. The *New York Times* on 12 July ran an article titled 'The Last of Rarey's Horse', reprinted from the *Ohio State Journal*: 'Probably no horse was ever more generally known than the celebrated horse Cruiser, imported from England by J. S. Rarey, whose system of horse-taming was for some time the sensation of this country and in England...'

But this time, a remembrance of Cruiser would not be appearing in London papers written by Henry Hall Dixon, for he was gone now too. He had died in 1870 at the age of forty-eight, after a long struggle with asthma. He had suffered so in the last few years that he told his son, 'Don't grieve, I shall be the happiest man at my funeral.'

22

LEGACY

'THIS evening we are to hear Mr Rarey's last lecture', said the *Philadelphia Inquirer* on 14 February 1861, 'and since Alexander the Great tamed Bucephalus, or the charioteers in the Olympian games astonished the elder Greeks, it is not recorded that any man has so thoroughly filled the public eye with exploits pertaining to the horse, as this distinguished lecturer...No meteoric and useless merit could thus charm and hold the public...'

On stages all over the world, John S. Rarey and Cruiser focused attention on the intelligence and anguish of horses. After they were gone from the physical scene, their message of bringing out the goodness in rebellious horses was twisted and garbled by imitators seeking not to help horses, but only to profit from them.

These men claimed to be gentling horses, while in fact they were using the same old battle tactics of caveman combat. There were plenty of these wolves in lamb's clothing and the label of horse-tamer fell into disrepute.

Captain Horace Hayes wrote in his book *Among Men and Horses*, that by 1881: 'the farce has been played out so often...that it makes me laugh to see the so called horse tamers performing in England, night after night for weeks on the same old cab horse'.

Hayes dismissed Rarey's work with a toss of the pen, lumping him together with the trainers who copied him, referring to them as 'patent medicine men'. His attitude was coloured by his contact with Professor Sample – a self-glorifying trainer from America who came to London in the 1870s. Sample followed Rarey's pattern of

177

Photo of John S. Rarey and Cruiser
(*History of Madison Township* by George Bareis:
reproduced by permission of the Ohio Historical Society)

advertising for aggressive horses and claiming to quiet them, but
Sample's system was warped with cruel practices.

His method was to tie a horse's head to its tail and then spin the
horse until he was so dizzy he would relinquish his vices. The horse
learned nothing but nausea from this insulting trick. Sample later
invented a machine to tame horses.

Another horse trainer hoping to find fame and fortune was
Dennis Magner in America. He studied Rarey's methods and said
he was 'thoroughly disillusioned with them'. However, he used
Rarey's system of straps with some horses, but his secret remedy
was his 'breaking bit', which consisted of a rope over a sharp snaffle.

As Magner explained, 'When the horse pulls, the bit is doubled
across the jaw, and the shock of pain you are able to produce is
really the key to success.' Magner proved beyond a doubt that he
failed to grasp the crucial point of Rarey's message – being humane.
Rarey wanted to spare horses from pain, not give them more.

In Magner's book, *The New System of Educating Horses,* published
in 1881 in Philadelphia, he gives page after page of hair-raising
advice. The startling contrast between the two men is evident in

their suggestions on how to handle a horse that has baulked or stopped and refused to go forward.

Magner says, 'Try the whip first by giving him one or two keen cuts around the hind legs. Ordinary cases yield readily to one sharp lesson but if the horse is a stubborn, plucky brute, unhitch and go back at once to the second course of subjection [using his breaking bit]. Now occasionally giving a keen cut of the whip across the tip of the nose, which will hurt intensely…the main point is to force the horse out of the habit on the instant…The true principal is to combat the resistance directly.'

He also mentions in this section, the usual remedies for baulking: 'Any of the ordinary tricks of twisting the tongue, putting cobbles in the ears and dirt in the mouth, really amount to little or nothing.'

A clear picture arises from Magner's remarks as to the reason Rarey always found a supply of vicious horses, and why he drove himself to keep lecturing. And too, why Magner related in his book 'Do not, if you can possibly avoid it, handle horses in the presence of spectators: get them out of the way at all hazards. A sensitive woman should on no account be anywhere near you; nothing will touch their feelings so keenly as seeming abuse to a horse.'

Rarey performed the majority of his training in public, and with many seats occupied by ladies. As to Rarey's advice for baulking horses, he stated in his book:

What a mistake the driver commits by whipping his horse for this act! Reason and common sense should teach him that the horse was willing and anxious to go, but did not know how to start the load. And should he whip him for that? If so, he should whip him again for not knowing how to talk.

A man that wants to act with reason should not fly into a passion, but should always think before he acts. It takes a steady pressure against the collar to start a load, and you cannot expect him to act with a steady determined purpose while you are whipping him. There is hardly one baulking horse in five hundred that will pull truly from whipping. It is only adding fuel to the fire, and will make him more liable to baulk another time…

When your horse baulks or is a little excited, if he wants to start quickly, or looks around and doesn't want to go, there is something wrong, and he needs kind treatment immediately. Caress him kindly, and if he doesn't understand at once what you want him to do, he will not be so much excited as to jump and break things and do everything wrong through fear. As long as you are calm and keep down the excitement of the horse, there are ten chances that you will make him understand you, where there would not be one under harsh treatment.

In the following years, Rarey's system continued to be discussed in books on training horses, sometimes with understanding and other times with a begrudging chip on the shoulder. A horseman on the negative side of the balance sheet was J. H. Walsh. In his book, *The Horse in the Stable and the Field*, published in 1861, he wrote with chagrin of 'the royal road of Mr Rarey'.

> The year 1858, will ever be memorable in the annals of the English stable for the success of Mr Rarey and his partner Mr Goodenough, in extracting 25,000 pounds from the pockets of English horsemen by the promise of a new method of breaking and training...I have seen Mr Rarey exhibit his extraordinary powers over the horse more than a dozen times, so that I am in a position to form an opinion. In his public demonstrations Mr Rarey always commenced by some introductory remarks on the natural history of the horse, in which there was nothing to impress the auditor with any great respect for his powers, and which was evidently intended to kill time...
>
> Mr Rarey is entitled to every credit for introducing a novel mode of controlling a vicious horse, but it no means follows that his process is equally useful in horse breaking...I greatly prefer the methods that have been in use for many years in this country...
>
> The profound secrecy maintained for so long, carried the public away, and as in the fable of the fox who lost his tail, all those who spent their ten guineas were anxious to place their friends in the same predicament. This is the only way I can account for the extraordinary conclusions to which so many practised horsemen arrived in 1858...

Walsh, like the fox with the sour grapes, freely throws those grapes at Rarey's work, yet his understanding of horses comes into question when he discusses training problems in his book. 'When the vice of rearing has become confirmed', Walsh writes, 'nothing short of severe punishment will be of any service, and the horsebreaker usually resorts to the plan of knocking the horse down as he rises by a blow between the ears with a loaded crop.'

In London, Rarey had received a lot of criticism in the newspaper, *The Field*, and in the foreword of Walsh's book he states that he was an editor with *The Field*....

Samuel Sidney acknowledged the growing disdain for Rarey in his work, *The Illustrated Book of the Horse* published in 1875, saying;

Rarey's reputation has suffered from the inevitable reaction after an extraordinary season of sensation, and it is often sneered at by writers who are ignorant of or incapable of comprehending the principles of horse breaking which he illustrated in his lectures.

The best proof of his merit is the admiration which he excited among the finest horsemen of that or any other day, such as the late Earl of Jersey and Sir Charles Knightly. When I visited the late Sir Tatton Sykes at Sledmere, who had passed his life among horses, he said 'it was well worth the fee to see Mr Rarey's manner of approaching an unbroken colt'.

Back and forth the controversy went, but no one could dispute that Rarey's success in foreign lands had opened the door for horsemen and women travelling and teaching in other countries.

His reputation extended down under as well. Charles Ferguson in his book, *A Half a Century in the Gold Fields*, wrote that in 1858 the whole country of Australia was excited over Rarey's performances in England, and how he had 'conquered all knights of the saddle'. Ferguson reasoned that horse taming must be an easy way to make money, so he went on a tour of Australia as a tamer. He had some success, but soon wearied of the flying hooves and restless audiences.

In the twentieth century, an Australian horseman who experimented with Rarey's method was Tom Roberts, author of the popular *Horse Control* series of training books. Roberts had been a riding instructor in the British Army, the youngest ever at age sixteen, and always enjoyed the challenge of re-training problem horses. Throughout his long career, he tried various ways of dealing with vices and horse troubles.

In 1921 while in India, Roberts was asked to help with an uncontrollable pony who had gained the upper hand too often. In his book *Horse Control Reminiscences*, he described what happened; reprinted here by the kind permission of his wife Pat Roberts.

I had decided to try Rarey's recommendations on this quite vicious pony stallion. A real menace, he would kick, bite, rear and strike out with his forefeet to get his own way. It had taken much effort and several men to get him to the Riding School. With this young stallion, my precautions included knee-pads and leg bandages. The Riding School had the desirable soft surface on which to try the system.

After the straps were on, the pony gave a brief struggle and was soon lying down. A few minutes later, Roberts took the straps off and 'spent a little time stroking and purring to him...and gently handled his head and legs as he lay there'.

The pony did not want to rise at first, and still refused after twenty more minutes. Finally a couple of men helped to get him to his feet. Roberts concluded:

> The use of the Rarey System proved completely successful, for it resulted in a nice pony with not a sign of his old arrogance and savagery. When some months later I was about to leave India for Australia, I enquired about the pony and found he had remained just a nice pony stallion – and one of the family.
>
> Rarey was a great horseman...and I believe Rarey was the first to take steps to use this 'something' in a horse's character that in certain circumstances seems to lead him to give up all inclination to use himself, even in his own defense. I have found since, that this disinclination to even attempt to move after struggling unsuccessfully until exhausted, is also common to some other animals. Evidently, cows, too, are subject to this reaction.

A clue about this may be found in the behaviour of zebras in the wild. Once they are caught by a predator, they make no struggle to defend themselves, no effort to kick or bite. This is perhaps a mental mechanism in prey species, so that the animal can mentally separate itself from the gruesome reality of what is happening to its body when being killed.

Tom Roberts is now gone, but his warmth, wit, and wisdom are going forward to future generations through his *Horse Control* books, with the help of his loving wife Pat.

Presently in Australia, the respected horseman and author Maurice Wright, who teaches the Jeffrey Method, has also mentioned Rarey and his influence on horsemen in his books on horse training.

Another current trainer aware of Rarey's work is Linda Tellington-Jones, founder of the Tellington-Jones Equine Awareness Method (TTEAM). She conveyed her respect for him as an innovative horseman, yet was very concerned about people trying his method today. It is very dangerous to lay a horse down and, she says, 'It causes an instinctive reaction which makes the horse become immobile and submissive, and accept the one who put it there as dominant. Our focus is to take horses beyond their instinctive responses and reach another level of their intelligence'.

Rarey would have wholeheartedly embraced these improvements.

Portrait of John S. Rarey
(Courtesy of Mrs Elsie Rarey, Thornville, Ohio)

For as he wrote in his book: 'The only science that has ever existed in the world relative to the breaking of horses, that has been of any value, is that method which, taking them in their native state, improves their intelligence…for everything that we get him to do of his own accord, without force, must be accomplished by conveying our ideas to his mind.'

In the middle of the nineteenth century, when many people did not believe horses had a mind or could even feel pain, this was an unusual viewpoint to champion, but John S. Rarey was an unusual man. He was however, a real man, with problems, humiliations, and shortcomings like anyone else. People frustrated him more than horses, and he could show it in a quick burst of anger at times. But with horses, his patience was endless, for he felt they weren't responsible for their faults – they weren't kicking at him, but at the hatred and abuse they'd experienced.

He never looked down on horses for their fears or equated their fright with stupidity. He believed there was a reason nature gave them their responses, and it was the person's job to work with, and not against, the horse's best qualities.

Rarey wasn't a saint, rather a quite extraordinary fellow who was driven by a compelling compassion for horses, and the desire to share his view of the truth about horses with one and all. As he said to the London RSPCA in 1860:

> I am quite certain of this, that friendship can be thoroughly established between the man and the horse. My constant endeavor has been and will be, in every exhibition I may conduct, to show to the world, and to convince them by demonstrations, that kindness, of all other means, is the best mode of training the horse.

$\mathscr{A}$FTERWORD

$\mathscr{R}$AREY's house in Groveport, in the early years of the twentieth century, changed hands several times and eventually became the Hotel Elmont. In the era from 1910 to the 1930s, wedding parties, balls and dances were held there.

Mrs Elsie Rarey, an historian whose husband William is related to John Rarey's brother, William H., remembers the 'large square

The Hotel Elmont, Groveport, Ohio
(Courtesy of Mrs Elsie Rarey, Thornville, Ohio)

rooms' and the lively parties at the Elmont.

By the late 1940s, the music and footsteps were gone, and the house was silent and empty once again. Plans were made to build an addition to the school there, so the local school board purchased the property. In the autumn of 1950, Rarey's house was scheduled to be taken down. Some people in the area saved some mementoes from the house before the bulldozers came; including a black marble fireplace and the painting that had always hung on the walls, the 1860 portrait of Cruiser and Rarey by Miner Kellogg.

The Ohio Historical Society in Columbus presently has the painting in safe keeping. They also have in their collections: Cruiser's iron and leather muzzle, the wooden bit that kept him from biting strangers, and an ornamental netting of a deep purple maroon colour that was sometimes placed on Cruiser when he went on stage.

Information about Cruiser has been passed down through the family, and it has been told that his stable was about one hundred feet from the house. Cruiser was buried approximately nine feet from the stable, according to Ed Rarey, also a descendent of John's brother William H. Ed Rarey grew up in Groveport, and has raised a family there with his wife Anne.

Another family member, who throughout her life was dedicated to preserving the memory of Rarey and Cruiser, was Sara Lowe Brown. She was undoubtedly raised with vivid tales of them, because her mother was Elizabeth Williams Lowe, who assisted Rarey after his stroke. Elizabeth later married Thomas Laurence Lowe, and had two children Sara and James.

In 1916, Sara Lowe Brown authored a book entitled *Rarey, the Horse's Master and Friend*, working from Rarey's diaries and newspaper articles. She wrote another book in 1925, *The Horse Cruiser and the Rarey Method of Training Horses*. She lived on a farm just east of Groveport, where she enjoyed raising Shetland ponies. At the age of eighty in 1952, she was planning a third book about Rarey but it was never published. She died on 28 January 1957.

Groveport today is a quiet town of neat well-kept houses, and the people there radiate a friendly welcome. Main and Front-Street are tree lined, and the brick Town Hall has the large windows and distinctive character of a more graceful age. Inside, in the room used for town meetings, is a large portrait in an oval frame of John S. Rarey. The portrait was discovered, according to Anne Rarey,

The Town Hall, Groveport (Photo by author)

years ago rolled up in someone's attic.

At the school built on the site of Rarey's property, the Groveport Madison Freshman School, a large drawing of Cruiser is displayed in the office. The principal Tom Tussing said that when he tells the students about Cruiser's story, 'it really gets them humming'. The school's sports teams are known as the Cruisers. The land behind the school where Cruiser's stable was, remains rolling fields rimmed with trees, and beyond is a winding water way.

A few blocks away is the Groveport village cemetery, where John Rarey is buried. Standing at the back of the cemetery is a marble stone resembling a small Roman column. Rarey's name and that of his mother, father and the children who died so young are inscribed upon it. Alongside are a row of straight rounded stones with each of their names as well.

Rarey's resting place (Photo by author)

I visited the cemetery on a cold grey windy day at the beginning of April. It's a very quiet spot, dotted with beautiful old trees.

Out by the road, I saw a sign, explaining briefly about Groveport, and that a monument here honours local resident John S. Rarey, 'internationally known horse trainer and owner of the famous horse Cruiser'. Thinking of him standing by the paddock, watching Cruiser galloping with the sheer joy of being in the sunshine, the words that Henry David Thoreau wrote in 1842 came to mind:

'horses at present work too exclusively for men, rarely men for horses'.

$\mathcal{F}$OR FURTHER READING

Blake, Henry. *Thinking with Horses*. London: Souvenir Press Ltd, 1977. Paperback edition, Trafalgar Square Publishing, North Pomfret, Vermont, 1993.

Haworth, Josephine. *The Horsemasters: The Secret of Understanding Horses*. London: Methuen Ltd, 1983.

Holt, William. *Ride a White Horse*. New York: E. P. Dutton, 1967.

Roads, Michael. *Talking with Nature*. Tiburon, California: H. J. Kramer, 1987. In Australia by Night Owl Pty Ltd, 1985.

Roberts, Tom. *Horse Control Reminiscences*. Richmond, Australia: T. A. and P. A. Roberts, 241 Richmond Road, Richmond, Australia 5033, 1984.

Smith, Penelope. *Animals...Our Return to Wholeness*. Point Reyes, California: Pegasus Publications, 1993.

Strachey, Lytton. *Queen Victoria*. Great Britain: Bloomsbury Publishing Ltd, 1987. Originally published 1921.

Williams, Moyra. *Horse Psychology*. Hollywood, California: Wilshire Book Company.

$\mathscr{S}$ELECTED BIBLIOGRAPHY

Bareis, George Frederick. *History of Madison Township*. Canal Winchester, Ohio: George Bareis, 1902.

Bennett, Daphne. *Vicky: Princess Royal of England and German Empress*. New York: St Martin's Press, 1971.

Bentley, Nicholas. *The Victorian Scene*. London: Weidenfeld and Nicolson, 1968.

Booth, J. B. *Bits of Character: A Life of Henry Hall Dixon, The Druid*. London: Hutchinson and Co., 1936.

Brereton, John M. *The Horse in War*. New York: Arco Publishing Co., 1976.

Brooks, Noah. *Washington in Lincoln's Time*. New York: Rinehart, 1958.

Brown, Sara Lowe. *Rarey, The Horse's Master and Friend*. Columbus, Ohio: F. J. Heer and Co., 1916.

   The Horse Cruiser and the Rarey Method of Training Horses. Columbus, Ohio: F. J. Heer and Co., 1925.

Buchanan, Lamont. *Ships of Steam*. New York: McGraw Hill, 1956.

Campbell, Judith. *Royalty on Horseback*. New York: Doubleday, 1975.

Culhane, John. *The American Circus: An Illustrated History*. New York: Henry Holt and Co., 1990.

De Vries, Leonard. *Panorama: 1842–1865*. Boston: Houghton Mifflin, 1969.

Downey, Fairfax. *Famous Horses of the Civil War*. New York: Thomas Nelson and Sons, 1959.

Ehrlich, Blake. *London on the Thames*. Boston: Little, Brown and Co., 1966.

Foster, Allen. *Eyes and Ears of the Civil War*. New York: Criterion Books, 1963.

Gosling, Nigel. *Leningrad*. New York: E. P. Dutton, 1965.

Hayes, M. Horace. *Among Men and Horses*. London: 1894.

Hoehling, Mary. *Thaddeus Lowe: America's One Man Air Corps*. New York: Messner, 1958.

Howard, Robert West. *The Horse in America*. Chicago: Follett, 1965.

Johnson, James. *Horsemen, Blue and Gray*. New York: Oxford University Press, 1960.

Jones, Michael Wynn. *The Cartoon History of Britain*. New York: Macmillan 1973.

Langdon, William Chauncy. *Everyday Things in American Life 1776–1876*. New York: Chas. Scribner's and Sons, 1941.

Lawford, James. *Cavalry*. New York: Bobbs-Merrill Co., 1976.

Longford, Elizabeth. *Victoria R. I.* New York: Harper and Row, 1973.

MacAllister, Copeland. *Uncle Gus and the Circus*. Framingham, Massachusetts: Copeland MacAllister, 1984.

MacClintock, Dorcas. *A Natural History of Zebras*. New York: Scribner's, 1976.

Magner, Dennis. *The New System of Educating Horses*. Philadelphia: Burk and M'Fetridge, 1881.

Magri, Countess Lavinia. *The Autobiography of Mrs Tom Thumb*. Hamden, Connecticut: Archon Books, 1979.

May, Earl Chapin. *The Circus from Rome to Ringling*. New York: Dover Publications, 1963.

Offutt, Denton. *The Educated Horse*. Washington: 1854.

Photographic History of the Civil War. New York: The Fairfax Press, 1989.

Powell, Willis J. *Tachyhippodamia: The New Secret of Taming Horses*. Philadelphia: Hubbard Bros. Publishers, 1877.

Rarey, John S. *The Modern Art of Taming Wild Horses*. Columbus, Ohio: Ohio State Journal Co., 1855.

   Rarey's Art of Taming Horses. Additional Chapters by Samuel Sidney. London: Routledge, Warnes and Routledge, 1858.

Sidney, Samuel. *The Illustrated Book of the Horse*. London: 1875.

Tallmadge, Frank. *Horseback Riding In and Around Columbus, 1774–1924*. Columbus, Ohio: The Columbus Riding Club, 1925.

Verney, Peter. *Here Comes the Circus*. New York: Paddington Press, 1978.

Walsh, J. H. *The Horse in the Stable and the Field*. London: Routledge, 1861.

PERIODICALS

American Phrenological Journal. 'J. S. Rarey Phrenological Character and Biography', March 1861.

Cregier, Sharon. *The Cruiser Courier*, 1975–7.

Henderson, R. W. 'The Great American Horse Tamer'. *Bookman's Holiday*, 1943.

Kearney, Deborah. 'The Man Who Hypnotized Horses'. *Highlights for Children*, June 1990.

Livestock Journal. 'J. S. Rarey: The King of the Horse Tamers'. Sept. 1927.

McCarthy, Tom. 'The Man Who Could Talk To Horses'. *American Heritage*, April 1969.

Ohio Progress Magazine. 'The World's Most Famous Horseman was an Ohioan'. Sept. 1929.

Sporting Magazine. London, 1857–66.
Thorpe, T. B. 'Rarey the Horse Tamer'. *Harper's New Monthly Magazine,*
    April 1861.

NEWSPAPERS
Baltimore American and Commercial Advertizer. Baltimore, Maryland, 1861.
Baltimore Sun. Baltimore, Maryland, 1861.
Boston Herald. Boston, Massachusetts, 1865.
Bridgeport Evening Standard. Bridgeport, Connecticut, 1865.
Cincinnati Enquirer. Cincinnati, Ohio, 1850.
Cleveland Herald: Cleveland Leader; Cleveland Plain Dealer; Cleveland, Ohio,
    1866.
Columbus Gazette. Columbus, Ohio, 1861–6.
The Constitution. Middletown, Connecticut, 1865.
Daily Evening Dispatch. Columbus, Ohio, 1861–6.
Dallas Herald. Dallas, Texas, 1859.
Danbury Evening News. Danbury, Connecticut, 1865.
Harper's Weekly. New York, 1860–2.
Household Words. London, 1858.
Illustrated London News. London, 1858–60.
New York Clipper. New York, 1861–5.
New York Sunday Mercury. New York, 1865.
New York Times. New York, 1857–66.
Norwalk Gazette. Norwalk, Connecticut, 1865.
Ohio State Journal. Columbus, Ohio, 1860–6.
Philadelphia Inquirer. Philadelphia, Pennsylvania, 1861.
Punch. London, 1858.
The Times. London, 1858.
The Turf, Field, and Farm. New York, 1866.

$\mathcal{I}$NDEX